"Congress is the biggest glass house in the world when it comes to misbehavior."

—Maureen Dowd, "Liberties,"
The New York Times,
October 7, 1998

GLASS HOUSES

Shocking Profiles of Congressional Sex Scandals and Other Unofficial Misconduct

STANLEY G. HILTON and
DR. ANNE-RENEE TESTA

St. Martin's Paperbacks

GLASS HOUSES

Copyright © 1998 by Stanley G. Hilton and Dr. Anne-Renee Testa.

Cover photographs of members of Congress courtesy AP/Wide World Photos. Photo of broken glass with photos by Don Banks.

All rights reserved. No part of this book may be used or reproduced in any manner whatsoever without written permission except in the case of brief quotations embodied in critical articles or reviews. For information address St. Martin's Press, 175 Fifth Avenue, New York, N.Y. 10010.

ISBN: 0-312-97102-8

Printed in the United States of America

St. Martin's Paperbacks edition / November 1998

10 9 8 7 6 5 4 3 2 1

This book is dedicated to
"The Truth."

ACKNOWLEDGMENTS

I wish to thank the following people for helping me to put this book together:

My inspiring and wonderful wife Raquel; my brilliant and indefatigable co-author Anne-Renee Testa and her husband Les Tanner; my assistants Mavricki, Stavros and Lucky; my researcher Angie Brenner; my editors Tom Dunne and Barry Neville at St. Martin's Press; and last but not least, my remarkable literary manager, Peter Miller of PMA Literary and Film Management, Inc. These individuals helped put together this book in record time, with pinpoint accuracy and characteristic thoroughness.

My co-author and I relied on innumerable published sources, some of which are mentioned in the text. Acknowledgment is also owed to *The*

Almanac of American Politics, by Michael Barone and Grant Ujifusa, published by the National Journal, as an invaluable starting point for research on all members of Congress.

—Stanley G. Hilton

If there are any errors in this book, they are the authors'. I wish to note with great appreciation the assistance of my husband Les, Tom Guttman-Bicki, and the additional research efforts of Angie, John and Winston. Of course, Peter Miller not only obtained our contract with St. Martin's Press in a few days' time, but he was instrumental in coordinating the entire project.

A positive nod of appreciation to the entire staff at St. Martin's, especially Barry Neville, who saw to the editing of this first edition.

My immediate family, Les, Joy, Seth, Shari and Jon, were very supportive throughout, as were my early morning Central Park racewalkers, who shared their different views of the Clinton crisis with me.

My late parents, Robert and Trudy Testa, would have agreed with my thesis here that the genuine love from two parents when you are an infant and growing to adolescence is the best source of one's personal security in your relationships and your career. I dedicate my work on this book to them. To my clients who don't already own it, I say, as they already know, that by taking the best of what we did receive from parents and leaving the rest, we can change what we want and love who we are.

—Anne-Renee Testa, Ph.D.

CONTENTS

"Let he among you who is without sin cast the first stone . . . Judge not, that ye be not judged."

—Jesus

"There is no distinctly native American criminal class except Congress."

—Mark Twain

"If one were to eliminate from the Presidency anyone whose flesh is weak, the White House would have been deserted since the death of Thoreau."

—William F. Buckley, Jr.

"Dare to do things worthy of imprisonment if you mean to be of consequence."

—Juvenal

"He's not running for the sainthood . . . He's running for Congress."

—Remark about Rep. Alcee Hastings

GLASS HOUSES

INTRODUCTION
Casting Stones

This book is about what historians will call "The Constitutional Crisis of 1998–1999." It will not be entirely a correct term. The constitutional part is contrived. The crisis is real because politicians are using sex to destroy the President. This is new in America. Not the sex part, of course. Nasty campaigns have frequently led to similar charges and often, as in Senator Gary Hart's case, resulted in resignation or defeat at the polls.

Members of the Republican Party have officially adopted extramarital relations as conduct unbecoming a public official and think dissemblance in regard to it sufficient reason for impeachment. There's an important difference, however, between making it your own personal standard and adding it to the Constitution.

To impeach is to bring charges against a public official for specified conduct while in office. This includes all federal officeholders all the way to the President. Based on the history of misuse of power and the tradition of British parliamentary sanctions to check it, the Framers of our Constitution set forth what justifies removal from office: "treason, bribery, or other high crimes and misdemeanors."

Constitutional scholars interpret those words, in the case of the President who is chosen by the people for a fixed four-year term, to mean that the high-crime-and-misdemeanor must rise to the level of treason, bribery or a similar betrayal of the nation's interest.

To pretend that lying under oath rises to that level without considering what the lie is about would mean that lying in traffic court about how fast your car was going would get you fired. That is not real. It is not what our crisis is all about.

Let's get real about what is going on in America today.

The movie producers have known for decades that sex will sell. TV is onto it now. The Internet is awash in it. The books that sell in the mass market are of the Harold Robbins variety, or better yet the more explicit kind that started with Erica Jong's *Fear of Flying*. Madison Avenue caught on long ago. The ads we see for underwear, or even microwaves, are sizzling. Radio sends us Howard Stern and worse.

What is new about Clinton's crisis is the web that has been woven by three groups, which feed on each other in a national frenzy. First are the Ken Starr prosecutors with unlimited taxpayer moneys, accountable to no one, immune from removal, safe from having to testify under oath, who needed something to justify their suspicions. After four years of chasing the President for supposed corruption in office, the Starr team suddenly learned of the private sexual behavior of Bill Clinton. The result is the *Starr Report to Congress*, filled with the salacious details of the President's private sex life, an instant bestseller in the mass-media book market.

The second group in this spider web is the press, or what we now call the media. Their motivation is clear. Money and fame. The ratings, the newspaper and magazine circulations, the Internet sites, prospered whenever the subject was Bill Clinton's sex life. The very first time Sam Donaldson heard the name Monica Lewinsky, he predicted the President would be out of office in a matter of days. Tim Russert of "Meet The Press" has aired a parade of Washington "Talking Heads" or "Suits" who speak week after week on the subject of Clinton and Lewinsky. *Time* and *Newsweek* put Clinton, Lewinsky, Starr and other players in this sex "Gotcha" on their covers. The *New York Times*, *Washington Post* and other big city "papers of record" had the daily stories on their front page, above-the-fold; and inside were the editorials, comments and analyses from voices all over the world.

Sex is still king. It interests those who make no bones about their own sexuality as well as the people who do not want to talk or hear about it unless it can bring down the President.

We can all live with that. What has made this the farce that it has become is the decision of the Republican leadership in the House to jump on a perceived opportunity for political advantage. These people are known. They are Newt Gingrich, most of all, and Henry Hyde, Dan Burton, Dick Armey, Tom DeLay, Bob Barr, and Bill McCollum. Very few Republican members can decline to follow their lead, and none have in the voting so far. The power of the House, and the money, are in their hands. There are already Republican voices in the Senate, waiting for their chance to try a President they could not defeat in 1996; they are reveling in the opportunity to bring their "family values" and Clinton's sex life to their core constituencies. Trent Lott, Phil Gramm and Al D'Amato are examples.

It is truly a farce. Hypocrisy, Washington is your name. That official Washington dabbles in illicit sex is a "no-brainer." That many even revel in extra-marital relations has ever been recognized by the Washington press corps. That the press participates as well makes the farce complete.

Lies, both explicit and implicit, are regularly told to the American people by our officials in government. The sexual and private matters which they cover up are the most obvious. But not the worst. More damaging is the corruption which denigrates good government. Selling one's vote and influence for money—whether it goes in the politician's or in his campaign's pocket—is rampant. We know about it but we don't push Congress to bring about real election finance reform. It's just not sexy enough to grab the average voter.

Serious ethical violations which really damage us go on without investigation because the ethics committees are unwilling to expose conduct which is so widespread among their colleagues in Congress.

Special-interest legislation that plunders billions of dollars of taxpayers' money is made possible by leaders in Congress who place the national interest far below their own. We know about this corruption because it surfaces from time to time, as do the sexual exploits of our officials. The ones that grab our attention have to do with sex. That explains why this Presidential incident has taken on Constitutional overtones. It's the hook that gets this hot sex into Congress and on TV. It's not sex, they say, because everyone does that. Its not lying, because most people do that too. It's lying under oath: ah yes, that is how to hang this story on the hook of a Constitutional crime so onerous as to justify overturning the vote of the people. It's a good hook in that very few of the accusers, who have lied in their campaigns and in office, have ever had to do so under oath. It's a good hook in that you can fool some of the people some of the time, and you only have to do that to win the close elections coming up in a matter of weeks.

This book is about the hypocrisy of many elected officials in Congress, especially those who have been most outspoken about conduct which they, themselves, have engaged in. In most cases the conduct has been much worse in terms of the nation's interest. In many cases the discrepancy between what these officials say and what they do is even funny.

It is important in reading these profiles in hypocrisy to see the shades of character in these men and women and not only the deceit which our electoral process seems to require to stay in office. We believe that is fair to say that in the minds and hearts of every one of the 535 persons in Congress, there is that inner voice which says, I have not told the whole truth but it was necessary, though I cannot defend someone who is caught doing the same thing that I have done.

That, we believe, does not make them the wrong people to sit in Congress or head the country. History tells us that our Presidents from George Washington to Bill Clinton have lied. Many of them have lied about private behavior with women who were not their wives. The taunts of Grover Cleveland's 1884 campaign can be used today if the office is changed: "Ma, Ma, where's my Pa?" "Gone to the White House, Ha, Ha, Ha."

We already know more than we want to know about the sexual escapades of our more recent Presidents, including: Roosevelt, Eisenhower, Kennedy and Johnson. Presidential lying about Hitler's Holocaust, the atom bomb, U-2 spying over Russia, Castro assassination plans, the Gulf of Tonkin, Vietnam, the Watergate break-in, Cambodia, the Iran hostages, Nicaraguan Contras, the Savings & Loan debacle: aren't these of a higher magnitude than covering up a dalliance with a consenting adult?

As for our Congress, there are many men and women there who will lead our country in the next millennium, persons of extraordinary ability and goodwill, who strive to make America even better than we already are. These are persons of good human spirit and common human fallibility, who not unreasonably hide certain of their private and public actions. Hopefully the crisis we are in now will teach humility rather than hubris, and they will not use hypocritical contrivances to divide the country.

We see this crisis, which is a journey into the unknown, as being resolved by a form of censure or rebuke that falls short of removal from office. That is more likely to happen when the movers of impeachment feel that the political reasons for continuing it have been overtaken by the personal risk to their own careers.

We already have the stories of inappropriate sexual behavior among the Republican leaders. Newt Gingrich is reported to have had an affair with a campaign volunteer in 1976 and 1977 while he was married to Jackie, his first wife. The campaign worker, Anne Manning, also married at the time, said that Newt's preferred sexual *modus operandi* was oral sex so he could say "I never slept with her." There were other reports that Gingrich had extramarital affairs while running a "family values" campaign in 1978. Newt's response in 1995 to the *Washington Post* was, "In the 1970s, things happened—period. That's the most I'll ever say."

Senator Al D'Amato of New York actually announced to the press in 1995 his romantic involvement with Claudia Cohen, saying they were properly introduced in 1994 and they were both so in love that he wanted an annulment of his marriage. Al's wife, from whom he had been quietly estranged for many years, reacted to Al's unseemly view of his adultery and denial of their marriage: "An annulment—that's the craziest thing I ever heard. Maybe you ought to ask his bastard children about it." Claudia Cohen had been recently divorced from Ron Perelman, the chief at Revlon, and had a young daughter and $80 million which also appeared to be attractive to D'Amato.

Chairman Henry Hyde, the senior Republican running the impeachment inquiry in the House Committee, had a messy extramarital affair with a married woman for a long period of time when he was in his forties and a legislator in Illinois.

Chairman Dan Burton, who told the *Indianapolis Star* that he was out to get Clinton, is the head of the House committee investigating the President for taking improper contributions in his 1996 campaign. Chairman Burton's extramarital affair resulted in an illegitimate son he never publicly acknowledged or took into his home, according to reports in Indiana papers.

The number-two Republican in the House, Majority Leader Dick Armey, was reported in the media to have pressed inappropriate advances on young co-eds when he was a university professor and still married to his first wife. Armey's recent comment to the press was that his present wife is the only woman he can't say no to.

Republican House member Ken Calvert was found by police back home partially undressed in his car with a prostitute who was doing to him what Monica Levinsky says she was doing to the President.

John Peterson, Congressman from Pennsylvania, was charged by seven women with making inappropriate sexual advances. He admitted only that he was "too friendly" and an "excessive hugger."

J.C. Watts, the Oklahoma Republican Gingrich picked to give the TV prime-time response to the President's address to the nation, does not deny that he is the father of two children born out of wedlock.

Those are some of the Republicans who are casting stones at the President's conduct. There are also Democrats, and their profiles are covered in this book as well. Worse conduct is the lying about corruption, unethical legislative behavior, special-interest favors that cost the taxpayers billions of dollars every year. In order to present an unbiased as possible representation of these politicians, our book presents the members of the House Judiciary Committee first, an elite group that is followed, in alphabetical order by the rest of our sad parade of hypocritical statesmen (and women). Far from condemnation, we only hope to show how fruitless the moral outrage and indignation of these already-tarnished individuals becomes when placed alongside their own ethical missteps and lapses. In addition, we're going to take a hard look at the psychology behind these men and women, in the hopes of discovering what drives them to risk their high-profile positions with sexual and financial escapades, and we'll also examine the political marriage in the hopes of discovering what qualities are required for a successful one.

We believe that almost all of our officials in Congress have lied to the American people about something. We would all be better off if their lies were only about their sex lives. More often it is about money and power and corruption, about stealing or wasting taxpayer dollars. Such lies weaken the integrity and strength of our government. This book will explore the lies that many of our Congress members have committed by their words, their conduct, their misdirection about who they are. We present profiles of their often flagrant hypocrisy, not to condemn private conduct that is neither illegal or unusual, but rather, to make the point that the seriousness of the case facing the President has been wildly, and perhaps maliciously, overstated.

ANIMAL HOUSE
Sex in the Capitol

Before we concentrate on individual members of Congress, it's helpful to know something of the character of the Capitol itself, as constructed, bit by bit, by those who have served there over the years, including the co-author of this book, who has seen it first-hand. Sex is not new to Capitol Hill. According to former congressmen, House aides, and the officers of the Capitol Police, sex is frequently indulged in on Capitol Hill, and one can imagine these hypocritical congressmen, having just returned from a tryst in one of the many secret rooms of the Capitol, declaiming about the slide of our national character, or vilifying our President.

Former Senator Warren Rudman was elected from New Hampshire in 1980, reelected in 1986 and chose to retire from the Senate in 1992. In his 1996 book *In Combat: Twelve Years in the U.S. Senate* he tells of being a father confessor to senators who talked with him about their problems with women and wives who hated politics. Rudman says that one colleague told him that his girlfriend was pregnant, his marriage was a disaster and there was no solution except to resign. Rudman urged this senator to reconsider, and without naming him, says, "Today he's one of the most powerful men in Washington."

It is a safe bet that many in Washington know who this particular senator is but there is a code of silence that crosses party lines. Everyone knows firsthand the frequent temptations they face over sex, money, legislative favors, drug abuse, alienated children, and how often even senators succumb to these temptations. Extramarital sex in the Senate is pervasive.

The Capitol Police, who serve the Senate in the same way that the Secret Service protects the President, have seen sex in the Capitol firsthand. Former Deputy Chief James Trollinger tells of interrupting one senator with his brunette secretary when he was checking out his private hideaway office one night. "I knew them both," Trollinger said. "He was a big man. Everyone in the country knew his name. He was a statesman. They were naked and having sex. He said to get the hell out of here and close that fucking door."

Republican senators have been critical of the President's use of his private study behind the Oval Office for his sexual encounters with Monica Lewinsky. The White House belongs to the people, they say, and he has disgraced it. The United States Capitol also belongs to the people. It is a little known fact that there are almost one hundred private offices hidden away in that magnificent building which have seen similar usage by many senators.

These private offices are closed to public tours. They are identified only by door numbers. Inside the grandeur is striking. The rooms are beautifully furnished, many with crystal chandeliers, working fireplaces, long wall mirrors and decorated ceilings. Some rooms were formerly part of the spacious chambers of the nine Supreme Court Justices when the Court met there. Like Clinton's study, the rooms, officially, are for the Congressional leaders and senior members to get away from their busy public offices for solitary meditation. The Capitol Police officers know otherwise and some have been quoted for the record about former senators.

Just as four retired Secret Service officers guarding President Kennedy gave Seymour Hersh explicit reports about the dark and sex-crazed side of Camelot, several former Capitol Police officers have spoken out about the rampant sexual activity in the United States Capitol. Gregory Lacoss has told of accidentally walking into one of Lyndon Johnson's private offices when he was the Majority Leader of the Senate and finding Carole Tyler, a beautiful blonde secretary, having sex with Johnson on the sofa. Johnson was neither shy nor secretive about his extramarital exploits. He seemed to be competitive in that department with Jack Kennedy. When reference was made to Kennedy's appeal, LBJ is reported to have said that he bedded more women in Texas than Kennedy had in his lifetime. Of course Johnson was fortunate to have lived longer.

Joseph Califano, former aide to LBJ and former HUD Secretary, who was appointed special counsel to the House Ethics Committee in 1983, has criticized the Capitol Police for failing to follow up "significant leads" about congressional employees selling marijuana, cocaine and PCP.

A female page dormitory near the Capitol, at 235 Second Street N.E., has been nicknamed "Virgin Village" because young teenage underage female pages regularly disrobe with their windows open. Joel Raupe, formerly a congressional page at age sixteen, said he learned to smoke marijuana from the other pages, and had his first sexual experiences with female pages there. "There was a lot of drug use, marijuana, LSD, and cocaine," he declared. "We took our government paychecks and bought drugs."

In 1983, Congressman Gerry Studds (D-Mass.), who is gay, tried to force male pages into performing sex with him, took them out to bars, and the like, while Congressman Daniel Crane (R-IL), a conservative Republican candidate, whose brother had run for president in 1980, admitted to having a sexual affair with a seventeen-year-old female page, while married.

Neither Studds nor Crane were expelled from Congress, arrested, indicted or prosecuted, even though they clearly had committed felonies. They were merely "censored"—never expelled—by the House Ethics Committee. Neither was charged with statutory rape, even though it is a felony to have sex (willing or unwilling) with a minor.

Wilbur Mills, the Chairman of the House Ways and Means Committee regularly had sex with secretaries in his private hideaway office in the Capitol, according to Police Officer Wayne Beckett. One night he surprised Mills around midnight when he was checking the rooms and there was a naked secretary bending over Mills's desk.

Jimmie Young, a former Capitol Police officer,

will not identify the following senator because he is still in the Senate. One night Young and his partner were doing a building check and walked in on the senator having his sexual encounter on the couch with a secretary about Lewinsky's age. The senator asked if the door were locked and Young's partner said, "If the door were locked, we wouldn't be in here."

Elizabeth Ray, a beauty pageant star who later accused Congressman Wayne Hays of Ohio of paying her to have sex with him, was frequently in Hays's private office in the Capitol, according to Rodney Eades, a former Capitol Police officer. Ray was hired as Hays's secretary but said she did not know how to type.

Almost everyone on the Capitol Police force has come across senators, congressmen or staffers having sex in the Capitol offices at one time or another. It was hard to find a Capitol Police officer who hadn't had this experience, says retired Capitol Police Captain Charles T. Kindsvatter. One secretary used to "whip over to Senator Joseph Montoya's private office, screw him or give him oral sex and she'd be back in thirty minutes," a former Congressional aide told Ronald Kessler, who reported these and other shocking scenes on Capitol Hill in his 1997 book *Inside Congress*.

One woman aspired to bedding every member of the Senate, according to Martin Lobel, a former aide to Senator William Proxmire. "She'd almost had a majority. The word got out she was available and terrific," says Lobel. Another former congressional aide told of a lusty twenty-five-year-old blonde known in the Capitol as the "Attic Girl." She boasted of and hosted a regular monthly "gang bang" in the attic of the Dirksen Senate Office Building when "she just got horny." Captain Dave Curry of the Capitol Police said she was a regular with some of the senators.

Outdoor sex was also great exhibitionist fun for the younger congressmen who could not get a key to one of the private hideaway offices in their workplace. Congressmen and young girls would engage in all kinds of sex inside cars in the parking lots. Officer Linwood Binford, Jr. said, "You didn't bother them. After the sex they would kiss outside the car, one would go one way and the other went another." The outdoor sex was so great that Rita Jenrette told of doing it with her husband, Congressman John Jenrette, Jr. of South Carolina, on the steps of the Capitol. Somehow, as they were married for a while, this seems almost proper.

The Capitol Police are not talking about what is going on in Congress with the current members.

No one wants to lose his job. But just think about it. Starr subpoenaed the Secret Service agents around the President. If someone could justify sending subpoenas to the entire Capitol Police force, there would be mass hysteria in Washington.

The reasoning behind allowing Paula Jones's lawyers to question the President under oath was that it would show a pattern of harassment that would apply even if the sex were consensual because of the relationship of public official to subservient employee. Could it possibly be relevant in a Senate trial of the President to call the entire Capitol Police to show a pattern in the Senate of the same kind of consensual sex, the same kind of covering up, the same kind of misleading the American people?

No doubt Chief Justice William Rehnquist, who will preside at any such trial, would rule such testimony to be out of order. What is even more unfair is that the House Judiciary Committee has ruled that the Democrats cannot subpoena any witness without the approval of Chairman Henry Hyde or the majority on the Committee, which happens to be Republican. The same tight control over who will be able to testify in any Senate trial is likely to be given to the Republican majority there.

It is interesting to note, given all this activity in

the parking lots of the Capitol, that after Newt Gingrich's sweeping victory and the coming of so many Republican freshmen to Congress in 1995, Gingrich restored an old custom that had been banned. It is now permissible for the four hundred and thirty-five members of the House to "sleep" overnight in their regular offices, assuring them of plenty of nightime hours of privacy should they wish to succumb to the extraordinary temptations all around them.

Given this open and tolerated sexual activity in the United States Capitol and in the Halls of Congress, it is high political hypocrisy to criticize Bill Clinton's inappropriate sexual behavior because it took place in his private study. Would it make any difference if he had met Monica Lewinsky at the Pentagon where she worked, or even in one of the Capitol's hideaway offices?

If Senator Bob Dole has referred to Washington, somewhat in jest, as the "Animal House," then it follows that the ensuing profiles are a kind of guide to the various species that roam up and down the Capitol steps, preying constantly on taxpayers, nubile young aides, and of course, one another.

HENRY HYDE

Chairman with a Past Affair of His Own

We all know that Clinton's fate rests in the hands of the House Judiciary Committee, the chairman of which, Representative Henry J. Hyde of Illinois, will act as chief prosecutor of Clinton during the impeachment hearings in the House and subsequent trial in the Senate. But who is this silver-haired, seventy-four-year-old, morally upright, Bible-thumping Grand Inquisitor? Does his own background qualify him to act as Grand Prosecutor and Interrogator?

Despite his own skeletons, Hyde has promoted himself as a paragon of family values and integrity. He has professed shock and disgust at Clinton's behavior in the Lewinsky affair, and has led his Republican colleagues on the Judiciary Committee to endorse an unprecedented release of closed grand jury proceedings, including the entire videotape of Clinton's August 17, 1998 grand jury testimony and thousands of pages of explicit sexual details of the affair.

However in 1965, forty-one-year-old Henry J. Hyde was a handsome and prominent young Illinois lawyer seeking elective office for the first time. He had been married for eighteen years to Jeanne Hyde, yet he chose to begin an illicit sexual relationship of his own with a younger, more attractive woman, twenty-nine-year-old Cherie Snodgrass, a mother of three children and wife of forty-three-year-old Fred Snodgrass.

Hyde, who himself had four young sons, set his married mistress up in a fashionable, well-furnished apartment, unknown to his wife and to Mrs. Snodgrass's husband, and continued his affair for five years while serving as an elected official in the Illinois State House of Representatives. In 1969, Fred Snodgrass, having learned of the duplicitous, illicit affair involving his wife and Hyde, went to Hyde's home and spilled the beans to Hyde's wife, Jeanne. Hyde had lied to his wife and his constituents, euphemistically and hypocritically, calling his sexual affair with Cherie Snodgrass a "friendship."

What was the result when the truth finally came out? Did Representative Hyde come clean, resign from office, confess his sin, apologize to his wife, to Cherie and Fred Snodgrass and to the seven children involved in these marriages?

No.

Jeanne Hyde told Fred Snodgrass, "Your wife is a tramp." Hyde's affair with Cherie led to the breakup of the Snodgrass marriage in a devastating divorce. Hyde then walked away from his affair and his own marriage remained intact, though damaged.

Hyde never took responsibility for Cherie's disaster, ignored any rumor of the affair, and went on to higher office in Congress posing as a morally upright Christian gentleman absolutely devoted to his wife and kids.

When the Internet magazine *Salon* published news of Hyde's affair with Snodgrass on September 17, 1998, it quoted Cherie Snodgrass's former husband Fred as saying, "Here's the hypocrite [Hyde] who broke up my marriage." Snodgrass's daughter told the press that her mother, Hyde's long-time 1960s lover, considered the Chairman of the Judiciary Committee to be "two-faced" and "bad for the country."

Just before the story of his five-year affair broke in the press, Hyde appeared before the press to try and soften the impact of the disclosure. On September 16, 1998 he issued a public warning, criticizing attempts to gather embarrassing personal information about members of the House Judiciary Committee. He said it was an effort to intimidate members of Congress and interfere with the impeachment proceeding, and that it was a federal crime punishable by up to five years in prison.

When *Salon* reported the affair anyway, Hyde dismissed it, saying, "The statute of limitations has long since passed on my youthful indiscretions. Suffice it to say, Cherie Snodgrass and I were good friends a long, long time ago. The only purpose for this being dredged up now is an obvious attempt to intimidate me and it won't work."

This handling of the Snodgrass affair is pure mendacity. Hyde calling his former mistress a "good friend" is analogous to his more recent example of euphemism in remarks to the press on September 18, 1998, that his House Judiciary Committee's vote to release the Clinton grand jury testimony tape and two thousand pages of embarrassing details was voted on "in the spirit of bipartisanship, which is alive and flourishing in the Committee."

When Congressman Barney Frank, a Democratic member of the committee, interrupted Hyde to say that "Bipartisanship can't be unilateral," noting that all the votes in the committee were along party lines, Hyde countered by alleging: "I may have a different definition of bipartisanship. It doesn't include surrender to every Democrat's wants."

Hyde was born on April 18, 1924, in Chicago. Raised as a Catholic by Democratic parents, he came to see a widening gulf between his personal beliefs and social status and his political ambitions. In 1974, he was elected to Congress as the Republican Representative from Illinois' 6th District. Ironically, Illinois' 6th District covers much of the northwest suburban area of Chicago, including Hillary Clinton's hometown of Park Ridge. He has since been reelected every two years and is regarded by his Republican colleagues in the House as a man of integrity and intellectual honesty. When it was suggested by the Conservative press that Hyde act as Interim Speaker during the investigation of Newt Gingrich's ethics case, Hyde quickly stopped such a move on ethical grounds.

Today Hyde is one of the most senior Republicans in Congress. Chairman of the thirty-seven-member House Judiciary Committee, and the fourth ranking member of the House International Relations Committee, he wields great power in the Republican-dominated House. When he chaired the Republican Platform Committee in the 1996 San Diego Convention, he helped to retain the party's anti-abortion plank to the consternation of women across the political spectrum who see their right to choose as a dominant issue in national elections.

During his twelve House terms over the past twenty-four years, Hyde has easily won reelection in rubber-stamp fashion, winning sixty-four percent of the vote in the last election in 1996. His voting record is one of the most conservative in Congress. He has tried repeatedly to overturn by constitutional amendment the Supreme Court's *Roe v. Wade* decision legalizing abortion. Since 1977 his "Hyde Amendment" has banned use of federal Medicaid money by poor women to pay for abortions. Not surprisingly, he has spearheaded constitutional amendments banning flag burning.

Beginning in 1981, Henry Hyde, a former member of the House Banking Committee, was a Director of Clyde Federal, a small Chicago S & L. Clyde made questionable investments in real estate and the futures market, causing it to fail when the bubble burst. Taxpayers lost $67 million and the Federal Deposit Insurance Corporation investigated Clyde Federal and its Directors.

When the FDIC sued Hyde and his co-directors for $17.2 million for gross negligence, Hyde portrayed himself as an inactive director, but boardroom minutes disclosed the fact that Hyde supported the decision to engage in the futures trading, which was one of the decisions upon which the government built its case against the S & L. Hyde claimed that the thrift was still solvent while he was a Director but the record indicates that federal regulators repeatedly warned Clyde Federal that it was playing with potential financial dynamite at the same time that Hyde continued to serve on the Board.

Hyde resigned from the Clyde Federal Board in 1984, perhaps perceiving his conflict of interest but also clearly seeing the precarious position of Clyde Federal: the thrift was sending a lawyer and auditor to Washington in an attempt to appease the federal regulators about the problem at Clyde which later brought down the S & L. Later, in 1989, as the financial disasters in the nation's savings & loans were becoming more apparent, Congressman Hyde was a leading defender of the "goodwill" concept of inflating the assets of the federally insured thrifts simply because someone was willing to buy it for more than its net asset value. As long as an S & L had this intangible legal fiction called "goodwill" on its books to make it solvent, it could, by reason of this taxpayer-backed insurance, continue to gamble as much federally insured deposits as it could collect.

When Congress finally repealed the "goodwill" loophole despite Henry Hyde's defense, many S & Ls failed and many more were seized in federal court proceedings. One of these was the prominent Olympic Savings of Berwyn, Illinois, where Henry Hyde, Jr., the Congressman's son, managed an Olympic Savings Branch. A Director of Olympic, the now deceased Edward Madigan, was a close political ally of Henry Hyde and a leading Republican in the House who later became President Bush's Secretary of Agriculture.

Olympic's failure cost American taxpayers $111 million in estimated losses which were insured by the FDIC. It is ironic that President Clinton's impeachment crisis had its genesis in Kenneth Starr's investigation of Whitewater and the failure of McDougal's Madison Guaranty S & L. The man who is chairing the preparation of impeachment charges against Clinton was himself the subject of a 1993 government lawsuit over a similar S & L scandal.

There is a further irony. Hyde was able to settle the lawsuit in November 1996. Bill Clinton failed to settle his Paula Jones lawsuit when he had the chance after his November 1996 reelection. Hyde said he paid nothing to settle his lawsuit but has not said whether there was a company which insured Clyde Federal's directors and made a payment on his behalf. There was money in Clinton's legal defense fund to pay for a Paula Jones settlement but while the FDIC did not require an apology from Hyde, the Paula Jones lawyers did from Clinton.

Thus, in Henry Hyde we see a modern-day Elmer Gantry in action, a mountain of a man with his own self-righteous hypocrisy. His own scandalous behavior, engaged in during his hardly "youthful" forties at a time when the mainstream media did not pry into the sex lives of politicians, does not obscure the fact that Hyde engaged in exactly the same type of sexual misconduct as Clinton—if not worse, since he raided a married woman's life for many years and ruined her marriage, while Clinton briefly dallied with a single woman.

If, like Newt Gingrich, who insensitively divorced his cancer-stricken wife while she was in the hospital recovering from an operation; or Congressman Dan Burton, who secretly had an affair and fathered a child out of wedlock; or even Bob Barr, the conservative Clinton-basher from Georgia who himself went through two ugly divorces; Hyde sees fit to castigate the President's purported immorality, then his personal behavior must be considered relevant to his credibility and capacity to pass constitutional judgment on the President.

BARNEY FRANK

"The Incorruptible" Robespierre of the House Judiciary Committee

The ranking Democrat on the House Judiciary Committee is none other than Barney Frank, the irrepressible, bookish Congressman from the 4th District of Massachusetts.

Representing the Boston suburbs of Newton and Brookline, the 4th District boasts a cosmopolitan and intellectual elitism smacking of nearby Harvard.

Frank, first elected to Congress in 1980, is a Harvard graduate, a lawyer and a political scientist, who is now one of the giant intellectual and political leaders of the Democratic Party in the House. Political theorist, liberal poster boy and political pit bull, Frank carries great weight with his party and could be a pivotal player in deciding Clinton's fate in the impeachment process. But what about Frank's own background?

For years, Frank claimed to be "straight," denying that he was homosexual, and pretending to be at best an asexual Ralph Nader-type of ascetic fanatic, absolutely dedicated to the cause of liberalism when liberalism was under attack by Reaganomics.

From 1978 to 1980 Frank taught at the Harvard University Kennedy School of Government and ITS Institute of Politics, and co-hosted the public television program, *The Advocates*, with former Massachusetts governor and later Democratic presidential candidate, Michael Dukakis.

The Kennedy School at Harvard was and is Frank's core political base. It is there that he acquired the reputation of being an incorruptible Robespierre of the American Liberal revolution.

Once in Congress, Frank sailed along as an idealist for his first four terms, but in August 1989, he was caught with his pants down when the conservative *Washington Times* and the liberal *Boston Globe* printed a series of scathing news stories which revealed that Frank had paid for sex with a notorious Washington male prostitute named Steve Gobie, whom Frank later employed as a housekeeper and chauffeur for twenty thousand dollars a year. The article also disclosed that he paid for Gobie's sex therapist.

Even worse, it was soon discovered that Frank had allowed Gobie to use Frank's Capitol Hill house as a brothel for gay male prostitution.

Caught with the evidence, Frank quickly pled *mea culpa* and admitted failing to report his employment of Gobie to the government, and said that he had not even reported his employee-lover's salary to the IRS, nor withheld Social Security taxes. Claiming that he "didn't know I was supposed to do that," the Harvard-educated lawyer lamely apologized and called his misconduct, "a mistake."

Frank's shady relationship with Gobie began in April of 1985, when Frank knowingly broke the criminal laws of the District of Columbia by answering an ad in a newspaper in which Gobie solicited sex from paying gay customers. The penalty for solicitation of a prostitute in D.C. at that time was a maximum ninety days in jail and a hefty fine. The statute of limitations for this crime was five years, which had not yet run out at the time Frank's criminal misconduct was discovered in 1989. He could still be prosecuted under the law, but strangely he was not.

Enjoying a form of the infamous and legendary "Congressional immunity" (under the Constitution, congressmen cannot be arrested while in the U.S. Capitol chamber), Frank sailed on as if nothing had happened.

In addition to violating D.C. criminal law, Frank also violated federal tax law by not reporting the cash and in-kind salary he had paid Gobie for four years. Under IRS rules, an employer is obligated by law to report the amount he has paid to his employees. Frank defended his non-reporting of this by lamely arguing that "I assumed he [Gobie] was an independent [contractor]. He didn't have regular duties and I didn't supervise his work."

Like other members of Congress who have been caught violating criminal laws, Frank immediately dashed for cover behind the cloak of minority victimhood. He now flaunted his homosexuality, and claimed he was the target of a right-wing witch hunt aimed at discrediting all gay politicians in the United States.

The national gay rights movement quickly rose to his defense. Robert Bray, spokesman for the Human Rights Campaign Fund [the largest national political organization for gay rights] told the news media, "I believe there is a certain prurient interest factor [in scrutinizing Frank], and that is because of the gay element. In our society, the word 'homosexual' raises eyebrows . . . "

Bray claimed that Frank's political prominence in the national Democratic Party and in Congress, as well as his liberal voting record, had put him on the hit list of demonic Republican conservatives, who had leaked the gay prostitute scandal stories to the *Times* and the *Globe*.

Finding courage in this unexpected support, Frank now stood his ground, adopting an "Open Door" policy and allowing more sordid facts to reach the press. He volunteered information about the Gobie affair to the media: Yes, Gobie had been on his payroll. Yes, he had paid Gobie eighty-five dollars for an hour of sex initially, then later put him on the payroll. Yes, he had allowed Gobie to use his apartment as a brothel for illicit sex with paying customers. No, he hadn't known about the brothel operation until much later. No, he still didn't have Gobie on his payroll. No, he should not be charged with a crime or removed from office, because he "didn't know" he had violated the law.

Frank also pointed out that he had never used campaign funds or official government funds to pay Gobie, and insisted he had thrown his lover out upon discovering the brothel in his apartment.

Alexander Tennat, Massachusetts Republican Party Executive Director, said that the issue was not Frank's homosexuality, but rather his "profound lack of judgment" shown in the fact that he had "violated a law."

Frank's face appeared on the cover of *Newsweek*, and the *Boston Globe* called on him to resign from Congress. But Frank took an aggressive stance, called on the House Ethics Committee to investigate him, and survived. The committee recommended a reprimand, but not censure, on two minor charges. The full House voted 287-141 against censure in 1990, and 408-18 for reprimand.

As it turned out, Frank was easily re-elected to Congress and has been there for 9 full terms. In 1994 and 1996 he was unopposed in the primary. In 1996 he won 72 percent of the vote in the 4th District.

Coupling a powerful blend of gay victimhood with a *mea culpa* public stand and a pathetic claim of "selective ignorance of the law," Frank continued to serve in Congress with impunity, rising to become ranking Democrat on the House Judiciary Committee. One would hope that Frank defends his President with the same passion that others defended him.

BILL MCCOLLUM

Double-Dipping in Disney World

Congressman Bill McCollum is the Republican Representative from Florida's 8th District, which includes most of Orlando. In 1990 McCollum was the only one of Florida's nineteen House members to pay his top congressional aide, Vaughn Forest, $50,000 in "consulting fees" for working on his re-election campaign, while continuing to pay Forest's government salary of $82,500, the maximum allowed by law at the time.

Both McCollum and Forest told the press in separate interviews in late July 1990 that there had been no plan for Forest to take a leave of absence from McCollum's staff meaning that Forest was in McCollum's employ at the time of the election. Yet House rules prohibit members from using campaign funds to supplement official government

salaries. In 1990 McCollum, as did all Congressmen, received $441,120 for his staff. Using gov-
ernment funds for campaign purposes, as it appears
he may have done in the Forest case, is coming
very close to the line, if not over it.

That seeming disregard for propriety and ethics
had almost sunk McCollum before, in the Reagan
administration's secret Iran-Contra-Aid operation
which led to the conviction of Oliver North and
Reagan's national security advisor Robert McFarlane for lying to Congress about the operation. In
March 1995 North and McFarlane had met with
McCollum. North's notebook contains an entry
indicating that McFarlane had briefed McCollum
on the illegal assistance to the Contras. McCollum
said that McFarlane did not tell him what he and
North were doing, but what they wanted to do if
Congress could be persuaded to make it legal.

No charges were brought against McCollum in
1985. In fact two years later he was appointed to
the House-Senate Committee that investigated
the Iran-Contra affair. He prominently displayed
his zeal for the Contra cause in his sympathetic
Florida District and in Washington where the illegality of the secret aid was equally well-known. In
October 1990 McCollum's opponent for reelection, Bob Fletcher, called on special prosecutor

Lawrence Walsh to bring McCollum's participation with North and McFarlane before the grand jury, which was still investigating the Republicans' attempt to use money from Mid-East weapons deals to aid the Contras in Latin America. Once McCollum was re-elected, the charges for whatever reason disappeared.

McCollum was born in Brooksville, Florida, on July 12, 1944. He attended college and law school at the University of Florida and, after three years in the Navy, returned to Florida to practice law in 1973. He was first elected to the House in 1980 from his present district which extends from Orlando west to the Gulf of Mexico. McCollum has been reelected with wide margins ever since. In the House he is the third ranking Republican on the Judiciary Committee, junior only to Chairman Henry Hyde and another lawyer, Congressman F. James Sensenbrenner, Jr. of Wisconsin.

McCollum, however, is the lawyer, who the Judiciary Committee sends out, with his colleage, former prosecutor Bob Barr of Georgia, to appear on national television in support of the House's process of impeaching the President. McCollum's persistence and tenacity toward that end does not appear to be dimmed by his own earlier personal "close calls." Nor is he concerned about his questionable practice of having his travel tabs picked up by businesses and private interests. McCollum took a dozen junkets including trips to Germany, Puerto Rico, Las Vegas and Hershey, Pennsylvania, which were paid for by private interests, according to a June 1998 article in the *Orlando Sentinel*. It would seem to be the case, but does the fact that McCollum's transgressions are unassociated with sex really make him any less deserving of reproach?

DICK ARMEY

Flirtatious Professor Loves Politics

The fifty-eight-year-old Dick Armey is a large man of striking stature with a deep bass voice and a rough and ready sense of humor. He hails from Cooper Canyon, Texas, where he drives a red pickup truck, listens to country music, and wears cowboy boots, which become the black shiny kind when he dons his tuxedo for formal events in Washington, D.C. However, it's important to remember that despite his condemnation of the President, like Clinton this is a man whose charm may have been put to other, less honorable uses.

In the nations' capital, Armey is the second most powerful member of the House, standing beside Newt Gingrich when pressing the Republican agenda and helping salvage the Speakership after Gingrich's 1996–97 admissions of ethics violations.

Armey enjoys catfishing along the Potomac with Justice Clarence Thomas, the former Chairman of the Equal Employment Opportunity Commission, whose off-duty (some say off-color) talks with staffer Anita Hill almost cost him his present job on the United States Supreme Court. Justice Thomas's wife Virginia is also gainfully employed as a member of Armey's House staff.

Dick Armey's 26th Congressional District once included the power base of Democrat Sam Rayburn, who rose to become Speaker of the House. Although he has lately shifted the emphasis for his motivation, there is a story that Armey was watching sessions in the House on C-SPAN and it occurred to him that he could do as well, or even better than the politicians appearing before him on TV. In 1984 he got the Republican nomination without any opposition mainly because no one thought the incumbent could be beaten. As it turned out Armey won a close election with fifty-one percent of the vote.

For a dozen years Armey had been a Professor and then Chairman of the Economics Department at North Texas State University. It was there during the 1970s, when he was divorcing his wife, that Armey engaged in inappropriate behavior with at least three young women who were his students, according to Miriam Rozen, an investigative reporter in Dallas. Rozen wrote an article for the *Dallas Observer*, a weekly alternative newspaper, on "The Improbable Rise of Richard Armey" in 1995.

Then, on his April 1998 TV show, Geraldo Rivera flashed a video of Armey speaking about President Clinton and saying, "I believe he's a shamelesss person. And my own view is that if it were me that had documented personal conduct along the lines of the president's, I would be so filled with shame I would resign." Rivera thought Armey's statement was so self-righteous that he decided to take him up on his Gary Hart-like dare.

He brought investigative reporter Rozen on his show and asked her about "Dick Armey's alleged sexual harassment of three college students from the 1970s." Rozen answered, "Well, my impression was that there was a consistent pattern in that it was three women."

Rozen had interviewed his former students who confirmed that Armey was openly flirting with the young women before and after his classes. One woman, Anna, who requested that her last name not be used, was an economist with the New Mexico Legislature when Rivera called her in 1998 to check out the story. Anna said she left school abruptly because of problems she had with Professor Armey. She returned only when another professor, Cochran, called her to say that if she came back, he would personally supervise her master's thesis, reducing any pressure Anna felt about studying under Armey. She did return, had no more contact with Professor Armey, and later transferred elsewhere to get her Ph. D.

Another former student who gave her full name for Rozen's article was Anne Marie Best, an economics professor at Lamar University in 1995. She agreed with former student Susan Aileen White, who said that she took offense at what she regarded as Armey's inappropriate behavior with female students.

Rozen's article quotes another North Texas University professor, Bullock Hyder, who reacted to a question about Armey's flirting by saying: "Oh, is that old Dick Armey bird-dogging again? You know, Easter's coming up. Remember what they say,—let he who is without sin cast the first stone."

Armey appears to have ignored the Rozen investigation, a politically wise move whether in Dallas–Fort Worth or in Washington, where such behavior shocks few adults and even fewer coeds. One can't help but think of the letter to the Editor of *The New York Times* printed during the Lewinsky revelations, in which the writer declared that she and her friends knew many coeds who had their flings with older professors at college and comparing these trysts with the one that transpired between Lewinsky and Clinton.

With Armey's rough and ready sense of humor, he mischieviously alluded to these charges when a *Washington Post* reporter asked him in February 1998 why he finally bought a proper tuxedo for Washington night life. After saying that his wife had told him "I can't take you anywhere," he informed the reporter, "I can say no to every woman but my wife."

Dick Armey has an engaging combination of personal traits: the bluntness we associate with the plains of North Dakota, the seductive charm of the Dallas Cowboys halfback and the political resolve of a free market economist who can make a Contract With America and keep it.

"Dickie," as he was then called, was born on July 7, 1940 in a small town, population 1500, surrounded by the wheatfields of the Dakotas' northern plains. He was one of nine children whose father managed and later owned the local grain elevator company at which his mother was the bookkeeper. The desire to be the first person in both his parents' families to go to college occurred to him when he was eighteen, climbing electric poles at night in subzero weather.

Dick dropped the diminutive "ie" and in a burst of the kind of drive that later would vault him into the political firmament straight away earned his Bachelor's, Master's and Doctorate degrees. After four years as a teacher at Austin College and twelve years as a professor at North Texas State University, teaching economics, in 1984 he acknowledged for himself that professors teach and politicians do, and so the man from CAN DO moved to the center of the action, the constitutional branch of government that makes things happen, the House of Representatives. He was a strange bird in 1984 Washington, an apolitical who didn't even attend the 1984 Republican National Convention in Dallas which renominated President Reagan for his second term. The only person he knew in the nation's capitol was Democrat incumbent Tom Vandergriff, who he had just beaten in the November election.

Armey had little money so he started sleeping in the gymnasium for House members and later on the couch in his House office, something Gingrich reintroduced for the young turks of his 1994 revolutionary victory when they came to sit in Congress. For the first ten years in the House Armey was a back-bencher, and a non-ranking economist on the Budget Committee and the Economic & Educational Opportunities Committee, where he was frustrated and outvoted by the

Democrats he attacked for expanding government programs.

In 1993 Armey broke out by challenging the incumbent Jerry Lewis for Republican Conference Chairman, the number three spot in the minority party's leadership. Armey had opposed President Bush's ill-fated budget summit tax increase, which Lewis had supported, and this got him the votes of the freshmen Republicans who led him to an 88–84 win. The economics professor who regarded Bush's tax law as the reason for his one-term Presidency warned Clinton that the new president's budget and tax plan would guarantee him the same fate.

Now that Armey's 1996 prophecy proved wrong, he may feel that his vigorous support for Gingrich's impeachment attack is the way to vindicate himself. Armey joined Gingrich in 1994 to write the Contract With America and then to sell it to the Republican candidates as the way to take back the country. With the surprise victory on both sides of Congress, Armey got the Majority Leadership without opposition. He then proceeded to amaze the pundits by actually delivering the campaign promise to debate each provision of the Contract in the first one hundred days of the new Congress. What's more, with the symbiotic tenacity of the one-two Gingrich-Armey team, the House passed every provision of the Contract except for term limits.

Was it that old saw about absolute power corrupting absolutely which tripped Dick Armey after his impressive performance? In June 1995 the House Oversight Committee officially noted the unethical violation he committed by permitting an unauthorized non-governmental group to circulate a political letter on his office stationery. But not to worry. Dick got that slap-on-the-wrist treatment from the Ethics Committee which Gingrich received nineteen months later in a much more serious set of violations. Admitting a technical violation, Armey simply promised not to do it again, so the Republican-dominated Committee dismissed the complaint against him. No rebuke, no penalty.

What's even more indicative of his leadership's disdain for the Congressional accountability groups that present complaints of member violations of ethical conduct, the House later imposed a moratorium on ethics while a special "task force" undertook to rewrite the process. The result was stonewalling and an offputting of the investigation and consideration of all ethics complaints.

That Armey of North Dakota is now thoroughly politicized can best be illustrated by an incident for which he is now generally remembered by the Washington press corps. In an interview Armey was giving over the radio, he referred to Representative Barney Frank, the openly gay Congressman from Massachusetts, as "Barney Fag." Armey later apologized to Frank for his Freudian slip. Congressman Frank, who bears an uncanny facial resemblance to Armey, good-naturedly took no offense. When Armey was later mistakenly identified as Frank in a photo caption, Frank called him and asked who gets to bring the lawsuit.

Army replied: "I have to figure out which one of us should be more insulted." Ever a flirtatious professor in love with politics. But as we look past his considerable charm, we must ask ourselves: where will it lead the nation?

BOB BARR

Clinton's Would-Be Prosecutor

The Constitution provides that an impeachment trial of the President takes place in the Senate with the one hundred senators acting as the jury. The Chief Justice of the United States, William Rehnquist, will preside over the trial. The House, having returned the indictments, which are the Articles of Impeachment, designates its managers (prosecutors) to present the evidence. President Clinton will be represented by his designees to defend against the charges, cross-examine witnesses and present his own witnesses.

That constitutional framework has been tested only once in American history, the impeachment trial of Andrew Johnson, who boycotted the proceeding himself, declining to testify or even attend his trial. Johnson was acquitted by the margin of one vote. If there actually is a Clinton trial in the Senate, it will require the vote of two-thirds of those present, which means sixty-seven senators, to convict Clinton if all one hundred senators are then alive and present.

If the House of Representatives votes impeachment charges before New Year's (the flexible deadline suggested by Henry Hyde), a Congressman recently elected to the House in the 1994 Gingrich landslide is likely to take the lead in prosecuting the President in the Senate in 1999. That man is Bob Barr, elected from the 7th District of Georgia, right next to the Speaker's own 6th District.

Among the Republican leadership in the House and the members of its Judiciary Committee, Bob Barr is probably the most qualified to lead the prosecution. And he would like nothing better. More than fifteen minutes of fame, Barr sees that role as a starring one in American history—certainly more respectable than that of Lee Harvey Oswald or John Wilkes Booth, both of whom also forcefully removed a President from office.

Bob Barr came to prominence in 1986 when he was appointed by President Reagan to be the United States Attorney in Atlanta. In that job he was regarded by many as the "Federal Prosecutor from Hell." He went after publicly prominent individuals and successfully convinced the jury to bring in guilty verdicts which required a unani-

mous vote for conviction. One such target was the
Republican Congressman Pat Swindall, an unfor-
tunate name for a defendant if pronounced differ-
ently with the emphasis on the first syllable.

After six years of Georgia headlines showing
him as really tough on crime, Barr sought to vault
up to the U.S. Senate. He almost made it. If another one-half of one percent of the votes in the
1992 Republican primary had gone his way, Barr
today would be the senior senator from Georgia
instead of Paul Coverdell. The former senior senator from Georgia, Democrat Sam Nunn, retired
from the Senate in 1996.

Barr, however, saw he had a chance of going to
Congress in the next election by challenging the
Democratic incumbent Congressman in the 7th
District, close to his Atlanta crime-busting base.
He easily won the Republican primary and got his
seat in Congress with fifty-two percent of the vote
in the year that swept his party into control of the
House.

In 1995 Bob Barr was the twentieth of twenty,
but is now the sixteenth ranking Republican on
the Judiciary Committee which heads up the impeachment inquiry. Despite his relatively junior
status, Barr and his Florida colleague on that Committee, Bill McCollum, have been the most visible
on network TV shows pressing for the impeach-

ment process to proceed. Both Barr and McCollum were practicing lawyers but it is Barr who was the prosecutor of criminal conduct. Of the top three Republican House Leaders, Gingrich and Armey were college professors and DeLay was in the exterminating business.

In 1996 it was Barr who introduced the Defense of Marriage Act which defines marriage for purposes of federal benefits as the legal union of one man and one woman. That law is seen as denying constitutional full faith and credit to any state court decision that in the future might recognize gay or polygamous marriage. It has no impact on Barr, who practices successive marriages one at a time.

In private practice, lawyers have to advocate for a client whose conduct they would never emulate. In Congress, however, the voters expect their representative's personal behavior to reflect the policies which got them elected. In Barr there is a clear discrepancy between the two. Bob Barr is a stern proponent of family values but he has already been through two unhappy divorces, is not yet fifty, and is married for the third time. How ironic that a man who is a public and staunch supporter of family values would find such an elasticity in his own life as to be on his third marriage.

In the Clinton crisis, Barr has repeatedly supported the questionable notion that Congress has the power to overturn a popular election of the President because he lied about sex. But he has also said, "It's really come to the point of no return with the government taking so much power. I really have a tremendous fear of government taking away our freedoms."

Barr has advocated, though so far unsuccessfully, a constitutional amendment to deny automatic citizenship to a person born in the United States to foreign parents.

Although he was one of only twenty-six Republicans to vote against the reprimand of his neighbor Gingrich for the Speaker's admitted violations of the tax law and campaign finance rules, Barr was pushing to impeach Clinton for breaking the law long before the public even heard the name of Monica Lewinsky.

In his 1995 State of the Union message Clinton called for a law banning Congress members from accepting personal gifts from lobbyists. The President suggested that, until the law is enacted, members should voluntarily decline such gifts. Only ten percent of the Congress, forty-six in the House and seven in the Senate, stepped forward to sign pledges not to permit lobbyists to compromise them. Bob Barr was in the ninety percent category. He refused to commit. His chief of staff said that Barr follows a "good-judgment policy" and is sure he will not be judged to be unethical by the House Committee.

Bob Barr is close to the Christian Coalition, the right wing of the Republican Party and an influential member of Newt Gingrich's powerful cadre. He has been a frequent guest on NBC's "Meet the Press," ABC's "This Week With Sam Donaldson and Cokie Roberts," and other network and cable shows like "Crossfire," as an outspoken prosecutor urging Clinton's removal from office. It is his ambition to be the House's prosecutor if and when C-SPAN and Court TV provide live coverage of the historic "Trial of the President." However, his drive and ambition seem too strong to be satisfied merely by the position of prosecutor, and Barr should beware of his own past should he seek even higher office.

JOE BIDEN

Copycat Serial Speaker, Senate Zelig

When it comes to the question of integrity, and the "character issue" of whether one is an honest person who always tells the truth under oath, we would be well-advised to look at how the person in question behaves when he is not under oath, for that sheds much light on how honest he is.

People who lie under oath generally also lie when not under oath, and vice versa. The real issue, then, is character: integrity, probity, forthrightness. Does the politician have any genuine respect for Truth? Or, rather, does he side with Pontius Pilate in asking cynically, "What is Truth?"

For a politician, forever balancing his act on the tightrope of public opinion, the question is really whether the politician has an innate sense of honesty which shows itself when he is least watched—

when he is not under oath. If such a politician lies with abandon on the campaign hustings, chances are he will probably lie under oath if forced to testify.

One has to wonder about Joe Biden, the long-time lifetime senator from Delaware who is one of those old congressional fossils who seem to enjoy a lifetime seat once they get into the hallowed grounds of the congressional Land of Oz.

While Joe Biden's Delaware constituents may find nothing wrong with his probity, and may keep giving him a lifetime ticket to his Senate playground, the national media and constituency are something else.

Biden is a man who appears bright, articulate and Kennedyesque on the surface. Another political *wunderkind* who was first elected to the U.S. Senate from Delaware in 1972 at the tender age of twenty-nine, just four years out of law school, he is now one of the longest serving senators, having occupied his seat for twenty-six years, and is likely to remain in this sinecure for his entire life.

Today, Sen. Joseph Biden of Delaware sits as the ranking Democratic member on the Senate Judiciary Committee. If the Clinton case for impeachment goes to the Senate for trial, Biden would be one of the principal players whose recommendations would influence his Democratic colleagues.

But is Joe Biden qualified by character to play this role of president maker or breaker?

Just who is this faceless figure who has represented Delaware in the Senate for over a quarter of this century, and who still aspires to be President?

In 1987, shortly after Gary Hart was driven out of the presidential race with his "Monkey Business" Donna Rice sex scandal, Biden became the front-runner for the Democratic presidential nomination for 1988. He had a fat wallet, an attractive wife and family, and a reputation as Mr. Clean and Mr. Bright. He was also the point man on issues dear to Democrats, such as Israel, women's rights, gay rights and the like.

But the so-called "character issue" caught up with Biden in an obscure place and time.

If it is true that politicians are most likely to let down their guard when they do not think they are being watched, then Biden fell into this "character trap" on an obscure summer day in the tiny town of Claremont, New Hampshire, where his true character came out.

Running for President in the key primary state of New Hampshire, he lashed out at an anonymous member of the audience, and revealed an ugly, monstrous ego that ignored the boundary between truth and baseless hyperbole.

In Claremont, New Hampshire, during the bitterly contested nomination battle in September 1987, one of Biden's rivals (who to this day has not been identified) sent an anonymous C-SPAN videotape of Biden speaking to the news media, along with a message describing Biden as a pathological liar specializing in "creative autobiography."

In the videotape, a man in the audience named "Frank" asks Biden, "What law school did you attend and what grades did you get in school?"

This seemingly innocent question caught the intellectually insecure poseur, Biden, off guard. Feeling challenged and threatened at this arrow which he felt was aimed at his Achilles heel, Biden indignantly shot back, "I think I have a much higher IQ than you do. I went to [Syracuse University] Law School on a full academic scholarship and ended up in the top half of my class. I won the international moot court competition. I was the outstanding student in the political science department of my college [University of Delaware]. I graduated with three degrees from college. And I'd be delighted to sit back and compare my IQ to yours if you'd like, Frank."

On the tape, Biden appeared to be nervous and intellectually insecure. He also turned out to be totally dishonest. In fact, a look at the records showed that Biden had not attended the Syracuse Law School on a "full academic scholarship," but rather on a half scholarship which was based not on academic achievement but solely on financial need.

The records at the school also revealed that Biden had not finished in the "top half" of his law school class, but rather in the bottom ten percent (he was ranked on grades as No. 76 in a class of eighty-five students).

As for his college exploits, the record showed that he graduated University of Delaware only with a single Bachelor's degree in political science and history, not with three degrees, and that he had not ever won an award given to the outstanding political science student at the University of Delaware.

This blatant dishonesty, repeated in speeches all over the country, was also shown in Biden's shameless theft of autobiographical speech material from a prominent British politician, Labour Leader Neil Kinnock, as well as his wholesale plagiarizing of the speeches of Robert Kennedy and other golden-tongued orators.

Kinnock, the British Labor Party leader who criticized the British class system, tended to boast in his speeches by asking rhetorically, "Why am I the first in one thousand generations to be able to get to University? Why is Glenys [Kinnock's wife] the first woman in her family to be able to get to

University? Was it because all our predecessors were stupid? Was it because they were weak? Weak? Those people who could work eight hours underground and then come up to play football! No! It was because there was no platform upon which they could stand!"

Biden, in August 1987, during a speech in Des Moines, recited to an Iowa state fair crowd the following Kinnockian speech, which he plagiarized: "Why is it that Joe Biden is the first in his family ever to go to a university? Why is it that my wife is the first in her family to ever go to college? Is it because our fathers and mothers were not bright? Is it because they didn't work hard? My ancestors worked in the coal mines of Northeast Pennsylvania and would come home after twelve hours and play football for four hours. It is because they didn't have a platform upon which to stand."

Biden clearly lifted the speech from Kinnock and did not give Kinnock any credit. Plagiarism is the ultimate crime in academia, is often called the "most serious academic felony," and can get a student or professor thrown out of school if discovered. It amounts to intellectual grand larceny and to theft of another man's ideas.

As if that were not enough, Biden also went around the country plagiarizing many other political giants' speeches. One of his favorites was a line from Robert F. Kennedy's 1966 speech to South African students (protesting apartheid), from which Biden stole the following ringing words and presented them as his own: "Few here will have the greatness to bend history."

The intellectual dishonesty went on and on. In fact, it seemed that the more he spoke, the more Biden had to steal words from others, and invent more academic kudos for himself, with absolutely no regard for the truth.

When the media began prying into this hollow man's background, they uncovered massive evidence of earlier intellectual dishonesty and theft:

The record showed that when Biden was a first-year law student in the Syracuse Law School, he had stolen five pages from a law review article and presented them to his professor for a grade as his own paper. For this, he was nearly expelled from law school. Biden now dismissed this incident as having happened "almost twenty-three years ago." At the time, Biden begged the faculty not to expel him, writing to them that, "the fact that the opinion of the various cases I cited was not original, I thought was irrelevant."

Irrelevant?

Twenty-three years ago?

This is reminiscent of Henry Hyde's hollow

claim that his adultery as a forty-year-old was a "youthful indiscretion."

In judging whether Biden's blatant and career-long plagiarism is analogous to committing perjury under oath, we must point out that he presented someone else's intellectual product as his own, and implicitly swore the material was his. In academia, this is perjury and larceny.

Even though Biden has never committed perjury in a court of law, he basically committed perjury in spirit.

Who can seriously believe that such a dishonest man would tell the truth under oath?

For his part, Biden was widely censured by the media and his opponents, and was forced out of the presidential race in ten days, over his plagiarism and autobiographical dishonesty.

Nonetheless, he continued to serve as Senate Judiciary Committee Chairman, presiding over the nominations of Robert Bork and Clarence Thomas to the U.S. Supreme Court, badly bungling the Anita Hill-Clarence Thomas hearings in 1991, in which he was bitterly accused of covering up information that Hill had alleged being sexually harassed by Thomas while his employee at the EEOC. When the leaks about Hill finally broke out, Biden was accused of botching the hearings and turning them into a media circus, just as he had been accused of allowing the Bork nomination hearings to become a partisan witch-hunt.

Having personally observed Biden act in the Senate Judiciary Committee, the author can safely say that Biden is an insecure man with few if any convictions, a man who has no real identity and who needs to borrow the identity of others in order to say or do anything.

Biden's background may shed some light on his character. As a child, he developed a terrible stutter and a nagging inferiority complex. Ridiculed for his stutter and his mental slowness, he retreated from his own self and began to copy the voices and behavioral patterns of others. Like Demosthenes, he taught himself how to overcome his stutter by delivering a speech to his entire school. Unlike Demosthenes, however, he failed to develop into his own man, and framed his entire career on copying from others, assuming their identities and uttering their words as if they were his own.

Biden has always won reelection to the Senate from Delaware without any serious opposition every six years. In a Clinton impeachment trial in the Senate, he would probably function as one of the key Senate inquisitors calling the shots.

Biden is truly the modern day "Zelig" of Congress. Like the real-life Leonard Zelig of the 1920s (parodied and immortalized in Woody Allen's spoof, *Zelig*), Biden seems to be a man without an identity, who continually borrows the personalities and words of those he encounters, and who invents a false past for himself, and who has a knack for showing up in important historical settings at the oddest moments.

Is this Senate Zelig qualified to determine the fate of a president accused of perjury?

DAVID BONIOR
Conscience of the House?

David Bonior, Congressman from the 10th Congressional district of Michigan, has become something of a household word since the Clinton impeachment scandal broke. Bearded, outspoken, articulate and liberal, Bonior represents the "old time partisan Democrat liberal," and has differed from Clinton on numerous issues as Clinton has tried to coopt Republicans, moderates and conservatives. First elected to the House in 1976, Bonior is from east Detroit, the grandson of Polish–Lithuanian immigrants.

But in the House, he has risen as the Voice of Conscience, the most outspoken, combative critic of Gingrich and the Republican Young Turks. He has led the fight to file over 70 ethics violation charges against Gingrich in the House. Once asked if he respected the Speaker, he replied, "No, I don't. I've watched him operate for a long time . . . I've watched him violate rules and laws, and I've watched him tear down the institution. And I've watched him really tear down things that I care about for my constituents."

But how clean is Bonior himself? While marital infidelity and divorce rumors have haunted him, the more serious charges against Bonior have concerned improper conduct by staff in his own House office.

Shortly after accusing Gingrich of ethics violations for accepting a $4.5 million advance for a book deal from Rupert Murdoch's company, Bonior was accused by Gingrich of using his staff as researchers and co-authors of a 1984 book about Vietnam veterans, for which they received advances.

In 1997, the Republican Leadership Conference complained that Florida Democratic activists had illegally taped one of their phone conversations, which is a federal crime.

The Floridians returned the tape to Democratic Congresswoman Karen Thurman (D–Fla), who returned it to them and suggested that senior aides of Bonior had admitted taping the call and said they would get immunity from prosecution if they turned the tape over to the Committee.

While the case remains murky, Bonior remained uncharacteristically quiet for weeks following this snafu, and he even failed to speak in the well of the House on the day Gingrich was reprimanded by the full House for ethical violations.

Again, this seems to be a case where a congressman and his staff acted above the law, and got away with it.

DAN BURTON

Called Clinton a "Vulgarity for a Condom"

Dan Burton is the Congressman from the 6th District of Indiana which includes most of the suburban communities surrounding Indianapolis. Burton's 6th District is the most Republican in Indiana and one of the most Republican in the United States. It is ninety-seven percent white. Sixty-five percent of the households are married couples with families. Family values are important and Burton is an enthusiastic proponent of the conservative views of his constituency. He is sixty years old and has been in politics his entire life. In 1996 Burton might have been elected Governor of Indiana. Democrat Evan Bayh was stepping down, and Bayh had been the only Democrat to serve as Governor of Indiana in the last twenty-eight years. But Bill Clinger, the long-term Pennsylvania Congressman who was Chairman of the powerful Government Reform and Oversight Committee in the House, announced that he was retiring from Congress, and Burton opted to retain his safe seat and move up to Chairman of that Committee. Burton knew that the Chairman of that Committee was destined to receive national attention, because of its investigation into the Clinton White House. For some time Burton had been committed to "getting" Clinton.

Dan Burton, unfortunately, was not lucky enough to be born into the kind of family background that is typical of his district. Born on June 21, 1938, as the Great Depression was about to be saved by World War II, Burton had an awful childhood. His father was abusive and left the family. His mother was hard put to provide for her children. Working as a waitress, she bought their clothes at Goodwill. His father actually came back in order to kidnap his mother, but was sent to jail while Dan and his siblings ended up in the county foster home. As an adolescent, Burton experienced none of the warmth or familial support of his future 6th District families.

The United States literally rescued him. At eighteen, Burton enlisted in the Army and after his discharge in 1959 he spent one year at Indiana University and one year at Cincinnati Bible Seminary, while serving in the Army Reserves. Burton did not finish college, but he soon made his way in business as a real estate broker and insurance salesman, founding his own company, Dan Burton Insurance Agency.

While still in his twenties, Dan Burton settled on politics as his real career. He ran for public office almost every two years. His first victory was his election to the Indiana Legislature in 1966, when he was twenty-eight and two years later he won a seat in the Indiana Senate. In 1970, he tried to move up to the United States House but he lost the election that year and again in 1972.

Burton is not easily discouraged. He started up the ladder again, winning election to the Indiana House in 1976 and 1978 and the Indiana Senate in 1980. After the 1980 census and the redistricting in the Indiana Legislature, the heavily Republican suburban 6th district was created and Burton found his electoral home there. Assuming that seat in 1982, he established a feisty, confrontational style long before it became the province of the 1994 Republican majority, achieved by his ideological ally in the House, Newt Gingrich.

When Dan Burton moved to the Chair of the House Committee on Government Reform and Oversight he aggressively pursued his investigation into campaign fund-raising in the November 1996

Presidential election. Representative Henry Waxman of California, the ranking Democrat on Burton's Committee, has called Burton's investigation a "partisan witch-hunt," noting that Burton's committee sent out one thousand and thirty-seven subpoenas or requests for information, of which only about a dozen were aimed at Republican targets.

Issuing a subpoena is an awesome power. According to Representative Waxman it is one of the most invasive tools possessed by government, and furthermore there has never been an investigation where the chairman has asserted as much power as Burton has. In fact, Burton single-handedly issued about six hundred subpoenas in eighteen months.

Burton also was blamed for the actions of his controversial investigator, David Bossie, who publicly released taped telephone conversations of Webster Hubbell while Hubbell was in prison. Bossie rushed partial transcripts and edited versions of the tapes to the news media to support the claim that Hubbell, a close friend of Hillary and Bill Clinton, had received payoffs from Clinton supporters to keep him silent on Whitewater issues being investigated by Ken Starr.

Bossie's release coincided with Hubbell's indictment by Starr on income tax charges which were later dismissed out of hand by a federal court.

Bossie left Burton's Committee when it appeared that he had omitted critical portions of Hubbell's taped conversations that showed there had been no attempt by the Clinton forces to keep him quiet.

Burton himself got into trouble around the time of Bossie's departure by calling Clinton a "scumbag" in a meeting with the editorial board of the *Indianapolis Star*. In the same interview, he vowed to get the President. Burton's partisan animosity and his vulgar language so upset everyone, even some of his Republican backers, that Burton promised to be more evenhanded in order to keep the investigation in his committee. The *New York Times* had difficulty using Burton's obscenity about Clinton, describing it as a "vulgarity for a condom."

Burton's obsession about getting Clinton was clearly a mistake for a man who lives in his own glass house. Just as Henry Hyde was "outed" for his pious invoking of family values in criticizing Clinton's conduct with Lewinsky, Burton received his comeuppance for his own sexual obscenity. He was informed that *Vanity Fair* had uncovered the secret about his illegitimate son and would print the story in its next issue.

On Monday, September 1, 1998, expecting the disclosure, Burton set up his defense. He told gatherings at two town meetings that he wanted to warn them in advance of a story that friends of President Clinton were dredging up from his past in order to discredit him. Burton said he and his wife, Barbara, had separated several times and nearly been divorced. He promised that if unsavory revelations were made about his life during those times, "I will own up to it. I won't lie about it. I will tell the truth." Burton told the public that if they read about his private life and "you think Danny shouldn't have done" what comes out, Burton promised he would be entirely truthful and take responsibility.

Three days later, the *Indianapolis Star* reported that Burton had admitted that he had had an extramarital relationship in the early 1980s and had fathered a child. The affair took place when Burton served in the Indiana Senate and the woman worked for a state agency. Burton insisted he wanted to go public, take the full criticism and deflect public attention from the woman with whom he had the affair, their teenage son and the woman's family members. Burton ended his promise to tell the truth by saying, "I have been straight as an arrow in my public duty. But this is private."

Burton's arrow was not so straight even before the disclosure of his illegitimate son. In April 1997, he was caught after accepting illegal campaign contributions from Sikh temples, which are barred from financing elected officials' campaigns. Moreover, Burton was supporting legislation in the House favorable to the Sikh donors. Once caught, Burton returned the contributions, saying that he really didn't need the money because his district is so strongly Republican that he easily wins reelection. One month later, he had more trouble with campaign contributions, and this time had to return them to a lobbyist for Zaire President Mobutu.

Burton was also investigated by the FBI for violating the penal provisions of the Hobbs Act, which prohibits federal officials from using their positions to extort contributions. A registered lobbyist for Pakistan has charged that Burton threatened his livelihood if he did not raise at least five thousand dollars for Burton's re-election campaign. Burton, whose legislative agenda includes matters favorable to Pakistanis, allegedly complained to the Embassy of Pakistan that their lobbyist did not given him any contributions when his threat did not work.

While Burton maintains that his failure to be indicted under the Hobbs Act is proof of his innocence in the Pakistani matter, his own campaign finance scandals are hardly the stuff of a straight arrow who is vested with the power to investigate the Democrats' campaign finance scandals.

But the story of Burton's infidelity is not quite over. Burton told the press that his wife of thirty-eight years has been aware of the relationship and that he had paid child support through the years. That appears to be Danny's idea of taking responsibility for his illegitimate son, with quiet payments which could also be seen as a way of keeping the woman from talking. Whatever the purpose of the payments, the woman is still not talking. The Congressman never officially acknowledged the child as his son. The boy's birth certificate does not list a father, and the child has a different last name. Burton has three children with Barbara Burton, but his other son was not brought into the family, though this neglect goes against the same values Burton proclaims to his district. It's comforting to know that this is the Congressman's idea of taking responsibility.

KEN CALVERT
Family Values with a Twist

The 43rd Congressional district in California covers Riverside County, east of Los Angeles, an area where Richard and Pat Nixon were married and Ronald and Nancy Reagan spent their honeymoon.

It is another staunchly conservative Republican area, and its congressman, Ken Calvert, is in many ways typical of his constituency.

First elected to Congress from the 43rd District in 1992, Calvert is a former businessman, restauranteur and real estate man who grew up in Corona.

A born-again Christian and a straightlaced family man with a cherubic, boyish face and smile, Calvert seemed the personification of family values until 1993, when his wife of many years left him and he turned to other means of amusement and satisfaction.

In November 1993 Calvert was found by Corona police in his car, half-naked, receiving oral sex from a prostitute and heroin addict named Lore Lindberg.

The Corona Police made no arrests and the incident remained hushed up until the election year of 1994, when Calvert's opponent Mark Takano made an issue of it and called him a "flagrant womanizer," and the *Riverside Press Enterprise* filed a lawsuit to force the police to disclose their records of Calvert's "incident" with the prostitute. The police report, issued pursuant to a court order, showed that upon being detected half-naked in his car by the Corona Police that night, Calvert had attempted to speed away to elude detection.

The woman in Calvert's car, Lore Lindberg, a twice-convicted prostitute with a heroin habit, had been picked up by Calvert on the notorious Sixth Street, a hooker drag strip.

Calvert denied hiring the prostitute for paid sex, a crime under California law. He also downplayed the incident. "I found it's a bigger deal in Washington than it is here [in California]," said Calvert nonchalantly. "In Washington, people live, eat and sleep politics. You come out here and people are talking about how we are going to make our mortgage payment. Here, people want results."

In walking the precincts in quest of reelection votes in 1994, after the incident, Calvert said he had "put that behind me," noting that "I've had a lot worse happen to me in life."

Though *Roll Call*, a magazine that reports on Congress, and critics called Calvert "the most endangered congressional incumbent in 1994," he went on to win reelection despite the scandal. His Republican primary campaign exploited his opponent's Arab heritage and hinted darkly that Professor Joseph Khoury was unpatriotic and un-American. He portrayed the Arab-American Khoury as a sinister stranger to the district.

As for his own sex scandal with Lindberg, Calvert claimed that Lindberg had flagged his car down and forced herself inside. He implied that he had just given her a ride and had not paid for sex. While few believed him, less cared.

Even tax evasion charges did not faze or damage Calvert in his home district. Soon after the prostitute incident, it was revealed he owed sixteen thousand dollars in back taxes on a nine-acre lot he owned. Claiming that he had "overlooked" this tax liability because of his "confusion" over his nasty divorce, Calvert apologized and said he would pay.

His opponents ran an ad against him featuring a cute song entitled, "The Liar," but Calvert won reelection in November 1994 by a whopping fifty-five to thirty-eight percent in the GOP congressional sweep, running on the "Contract With America."

"Think of the sheer logic of this," noted Khoury sarcastically. "What man would get flagged down on Sixth Street by a woman, pick her up and not know she was a prostitute?"

Calvert explained that he had been "confused" when he had "inadvertently" picked up the whore, because his wife had left him and his father had recently committed suicide. "My conduct that evening was inappropriate," he said. "Not because it was illegal, but because it violated the values of the person I strive to be."

Denying that he had committed a crime by paying the prostitute for sex—a rather weak assertion, considering California law—he apologized for being found in "an extremely embarrassing situation."

As a congressional clarion for "family values," Calvert now seemed the antithesis of the Moral Majority Man, yet the Christian Right continued to support him because of his official stands on issues dear to them: anti-abortion, anti–gun control, pro-life, anti-welfare.

In 1996, Calvert still found himself mired in personal scandal. His former wife sued him for failure to pay her alimony, and he countersued her amid a crossfire of nasty accusations of scandal and sex corruption. He refused to speak to the *Riverside Press Enterprise* on "any" campaign issues because, he said, the paper only wanted to "rehash the incident of a few years ago." Nonetheless, he again won reelection easily.

As in the other cases, in an institution where ninety-two percent of all incumbents win reelection every two years, it seems that local constituents are not bothered the least by scandal—whether financial, sexual or criminal.

In the strange world of congressional politics, there is life after getting caught with one's pants down, after breaking the law, after getting convicted of a crime and even after being impeached.

HELEN CHENOWETH
Hell Hath No Such Fury

Idaho has only two Congressional Districts. The 1st District is on the western side of the state stretching from the Nevada border to Canada and includes Boise, the home of Congressman (she does not refer to herself as Congresswoman) Helen Chenoweth.

Chenoweth is a divorced grandmother who was born in Topeka, Kansas, on January 27, 1938. She received her Bachelor of Arts degree from Whitworth College in 1962.

Before entering the electoral arena, Congressman Chenoweth was a lobbyist for timber and mining companies, living in a small mining town in the Idaho mountains, and earning a reputation for being stubborn but self-assured. She later worked in statewide political campaigns, leaving after a disagreement to launch her first race for Congress in 1992. She lost that contest to a Moderate Democrat when her core support from religious conservatives, sympathizers with militia and patriot movements and opponents of environmental reforms proved to be insufficient. She was swept into office in 1994 on Newt Gengrich's Republican tide.

Chenoweth's entry into Congress did not soften her seemingly impulsive but calculated positions. In March 1995 she openly met with militia members in Boise, known as the home of patriotic militias, and was quoted as saying that "we have democracy when government is afraid of the people." Later that year when the federal building in Oklahoma City was destroyed by two "patriotic militants" she said that "while we can never condone this, we still must begin to look at the public policies that may be pushing people too far."

One of Helen Chenoweth's proposed laws was her bill to require federal agents to have written authorization from local sheriffs before enforcing federal law, based on her belief that the FBI misused its power in the armed confrontation at Ruby Ridge. She was virulently anti-Clinton in her winning 1994 campaign describing the Administrations's environmental concerns about mining and deforestation by timber interests as the "Clinton war on the West." Having participated in the 1995 Republican tactic of shutting down the government, she was one of only fifteen Republicans in January 1996 who voted against reversing that strategy when it appeared that the public was blaming Congress rather than the President.

Chenoweth ran into her personal campaign finance troubles in 1995 when she admitted that she had not reported an unsecured $40,000 loan. There was also the question of her sale for $60,000 of land worth $10,000, which had helped to finance her last-minute advertising in the 1994 election. Her admission of the loan was delayed until after the deadline for bringing ethics charges to the House Oversight Committee before the 1996 election. In 1996, she beat Democrat Dan Williams by 6,500 votes, fifty percent to forty-eight percent, a significant drop from her fifty-five percent win in 1994.

Helen Chenoweth was an endangered incumbent in 1998 even before the September 1998 disclosure of her secret affair. In July 1997, Idaho Democrats charged that her rise to power in the 1994 election had been made possible by $70,000 of illegal campaign money from Hong Kong. This was claimed to be part of the $1.6 million which Hong Kong banker Ambrous Tung Young had funneled to Haley Barbour, Chairman of the Republican National Committee.

Taking advantage of the unrelenting Republican assault on the President over "Lewinskygate," Chenoweth has called the Clinton affair a "sorry spectacle" and launched into her 1998 re-election campaign saying that "personal conduct and integrity does matter" in voting for candidates for public office. In a television commercial, against the backdrop of American and Idaho flags, Chenowith spoke out against Clinton's admitted relationship with intern Lewinsky and rhetorically asked her opponent, Democrat Dan Williams whom she barely defeated in 1996, "Where do you stand, Dan?"

Before Dan Williams could respond publicly, her former lover's wife, angry over that television commercial, revealed to the press that Chenoweth had carried on a long-term affair with her husband. On September 10, 1998, Chenoweth conceded that she had carried on a six-year affair with a married man who was once her business partner. She said that both lovers had decided to put their families first and put the relationship behind them. Then she threw out the "Gary Hart" challenge, saying that now that she is a public official anyone who can follow me around will be utterly bored with my social life because I am one hundred percent devoted to my public duty. However, it's unlikely she would be so discriminating with someone else's shortcomings. It remains clear that Chenoweth has had little practice in what she preaches.

Her opponent Dan Williams finally tried to put the issue to rest: "My sense is that the people out here care a lot more about real issues that affect their families' lives than they do about anyone's personal life, whether it's Helen Chenoweth's or Bill Clinton's." Though many wish that were true, there are many in Washington striving to convince us otherwise.

ALFONSE D'AMATO
Senator Pothole Meets Gun Control Godzilla

Senator D'Amato says that the impeachment of the President is not about sex but about lying under oath. It is a hard sell to New Yorkers who have difficulty separating the lying from the sex. Many of his constituents have been there themselves. The question is how will he handle this hot issue in his close contest for a fourth term. Initially he steered clear, saying he may be one of the jurors in a Senate trial. That could be enough to defeat him.

The "sexual purity" issue poses the same problem for D'Amato as the "abortion" issue. A somewhat anti-abortion stance is a litmus test for keeping his core Republican support but it is a major impediment to winning the general election.

The impeachment case was initially built only around sex, not Whitewater, Travelgate, Filegate or the matters Starr was to investigate. The position that the President must be pure of sexual taint plays well with only a fraction of New York voters. If the polls are an indicator of how people may vote on impeachment, that position is falling in New York State at least faster than a lead balloon. D'Amato regrets that his Republican allies rushed out the Starr Sex Report to start the impeachment attack before the election. The public reaction to the salacious sexual details is the reason the Republicans insist there can be other impeachable offenses added by Starr to consider in the House.

The White House has decided to campaign across the country to win greater majorities in the Congress. Hillary first and then Bill Clinton have entered the campaign as if this were a national vote for the presidency, which it is. They are stressing the important national issues on which Clinton won in 1996 but the fact is that they want the electorate to know that it is important to get out and vote in this particular midterm election if you want to keep Clinton in office.

This underlying imperative has not helped the campaign of Senator Alfonse D'Amato for reelection in New York State. D'Amato is an eighteen-year veteran and a power in the Senate where he is

Chairman of the Banking, Housing and Urban Affairs Committee and a high-ranking member of the Finance Committee. He suffered a rash of negative publicity several years ago when he profited from questionable stock market investments at a time when the ethical question of whether members of Congress should be trading stocks based on information available to them before it becomes generally available, was raised in the media.

D'Amato looked to be unbeatable coming into 1998 because he had managed to build an enormous war chest in excess of $10 million and was expected to spend more than twice that amount to squash any Democratic opponent. In 1992 D'Amato spent $11,550,958 to defeat Bob Abrams, the former State Attorney General.

D'Amato is a pro when it comes to campaign fund-raising. He knows that the unofficial currency of Congress is the "soft" money, the millions of dollars given legally, directly and in huge amounts, to both parties. It is legal because it is supposed to be used to promote party-building efforts. In practice it is simply a good way to bypass the maximum amount individuals and corporations can contribute to candidates.

In 1996 D'Amato was Chairman of the National Republican Senate Committee and he transferred hundreds of thousands of dollars in soft money which had been promised to Senate candidates back to the New York State Republican machine. He told the *New York Times*: "There is nothing wrong with that. We don't have an obligation to tell people. Money is fungible."

D'Amato and his fellow Republicans on the Hill do not want to see the current investigation of Democratic fund-raising broadened to include their own activities. They are concerned that the examination of congressional fund-raising will show that Republicans regularly solicit contributions from their House and Senate government offices in possible violation of federal law as they have charged Vice President Gore with doing. D'Amato has already been rebuked for the improper use of his Senate office by his brother in connection with the representation of a defense contractor.

A bigger concern is that any investigation could suggest that some Republicans have sold legislation to the highest bidder and that the vast amounts of soft money given to them by special interests have compromised their ability to vote their conscience on important legislation. D'Amato, Trent Lott and the Republican leaders in Congress do not want campaign finance reform and they do not want the public to find out how they get their money.

The sexual purity issue is expected to work in

favor of the Democrats in the New York Senate race. D'Amato's opponent is Chuck Schumer, the 18-year veteran of the House whose strong record there and extraordinary campaign skills enabled him to win the Democratic primary over Geraldine Ferraro, the former Democratic Vice Presidential candidate, and Mark Green who lost to D'Amato in 1986.

New Yorkers like Clinton. He beat Bush fifty percent to thirty-four percent in 1992 and Dole fifty-nine percent to thirty-one percent in 1996. The sentiment for him to remain in office is stronger since the salacious details were released by the impeachment managers in the House. Most New Yorkers are not surprised about the sexual lives of politicians. They prefer their officials to be discreet and are not happy about other politicians using such personal private behavior for partisan political purposes.

They remember with distaste how Governor Nelson Rockefeller was treated by Barry Goldwater's supporters at the 1964 Republican Convention with shouts of derision over the circumstances of his divorce and remarriage.

New Yorkers are not unaware that Senator D'Amato was not happily married when they reelected him twice in 1986 and 1992. The stories of his estranged relationship with an invisible wife and having a separate bedroom at his home in New York were not raised by his opponents because his constituents understand his family life and do not see it as relevant. D'Amato appreciated this attitude and he did not hesitate to call a press conference in 1995 to announce that he was seeking a divorce because he was in love. D'Amato described in lead articles in the New York papers how he would be marrying the woman who had changed his life. Bob Dole was quoted on the uncharacteristic exuberance of his lovestruck friend who later engineered unanimous organization support in New York for Dole's 1996 bid for the Republican nomination for President.

It was a wonderful moment for D'Amato and as he knew they would, New Yorkers were happy for him with no adverse comment on how this had come to pass while he was still married. D'Amato was fifty-eight and his beloved was Claudia Cohen, the forty-five-year-old millionaire gossip reporter. They had met in December 1994 at a dinner party in Florida. By February 1995 they held a news conference at Manhattan's Water Club to announce their mutual love and devotion for each other. Ms. Cohen, an entertainment reporter in the "Regis and Kathy Lee" television show, was recently divorced from Ron Perelman, the Chairman of Revlon, with whom she had a five-year-old daughter. D'Amato said he felt like the frog who was just kissed by the princess. They would marry. The princess was a Democrat with a multimillion-dollar settlement from the man who was destined to offer Monica Lewinsky her job at the behest of Vernon Jordan, a Revlon director. A classic case of politics making for strange bedfellows.

About a year later, shortly after Valentine's Day in 1996, the *New York Daily News* suddenly broke the story that the wedding was off. Both Al and Claudia released similar statements that each was too busy to devote the time to make a marriage work and that they remain the "best of friends." Friends of Claudia made a point of discounting tensions between each other's social circles or Ron Perelman's attitude toward Al, as the stepfather of his daughter.

D'Amato's marital status is still "divorced" and he enters the race with Schumer, relatively silent on the attacks by his Republican colleagues in Washington on President Clinton. The last thing D'Amato wants is for his Senate contest to be a referendum on how the winner will vote in the Senate if the House impeaches Clinton. When he ran in 1992 Clinton's tide in New York almost swamped him against an opponent not nearly as strong as Schumer. He won a squeaker by one tenth of one percent of the votes after outspending his opponent by almost two to one. The close calls keep getting closer for D'Amato, and he's one incumbent who'll have trouble denouncing Clinton to an already jaded constituency.

TOM DELAY

Bagman for the Tobacco Industry?

Tom DeLay was born on April 8, 1947 in Laredo, the formerly wild town of song and cinema on the Texas–Mexican border. However, much of his growing-up years were spent in Venezuela where his father was in the oil exploration business. He returned to Texas, settling in Sugar Land, a name that perhaps presaged the success he would find there. It was here that he spent eleven years building his pest extermination business while also founding his political career. In 1978 he won the Fort Bend County seat in the Texas House of Representatives, the first Republican to do so in this century.

After six years in the Texas House, he entered the Republican primary for his present seat in the United States House from the 22nd District when the incumbent elected to run for the Senate. DeLay won the primary, the general election, and has been handily re-elected each year since 1984.

Much of his Congressional District is made up of southwest Houston and Harris County. The district is predominantly Republican, benefitting by growth in Houston and outward to the affluent subdivisions around the city.

On April 4, 1991, four-term Congressman Tom DeLay attended the first meeting in Harris County, Texas, of a new grass-roots political group, the Christian Coalition, which had been formed two years earlier after the TV evangelist Pat Robertson lost his 1988 bid for the Republican Party presidential nomination. The Coalition described itself in publicity handouts as "an issue-oriented organization, designed to mobilize and train Christians for effective political action. It is our stated purpose to reverse the moral decline and encroaching secularism in this country, and reaffirm our godly heritage."

Participating in that organizational meeting was a "no-brainer" for the representative from Texas's upwardly mobile, overly Republican 26th District, yet Tom DeLay's devotion to "reversing the moral decline in the country" was shaken less than a year later when he admitted in March 1992 that he had written at least nine bum checks on the House

Bank with a face amount of more than $17,000 producing overdrafts in his account of $5,300. Tom's *mea culpa* came five months after he insisted that his checking account was his private business, though it was no doubt influenced by the Justice Department's decision to investigate "Rubbergate," the scandal about members who regularly overdrew their accounts at the informally operated House Bank as though it was their private fiefdom.

DeLay wrapped up his defense by claiming that his wife had taken over most of their check-writing responsibilities three years earlier, and she did not communicate well with him.

DeLay enjoyed the politics of the House and he managed the March 1989 campaign of Edward Madigan for minority whip who lost to the junior Newt Gingrich by a very close vote. His virulent brand of politics later earned him a bitter reward. In September 1992 an editorial in the *Houston Post* gave the "Congressional Hypocrite of the Year" Award to DeLay for printing and mailing at taxpayer expense a newsletter that is "nine-tenths political propaganda and personal promotion."

Called his newsletter "a blatant insult to us all" that was mostly "a sermon by St. Thomas Loquacious himself on the sinful ways" of how "Washington is wasting our hard-earned money," the *Post* was also aggrieved about using the "family values" theme to attack the Democrats, with Tom actually blaming the Democrats for the country's high divorce rate. That was the year Clinton beat Bush despite the "bimbo explosions" which introduced America to the President's sexier side. Today DeLay is the House whip, the number-three man in the Republican leadership, and he is a leading "Talking Head" on TV shows, where he regards "family values" as a constitutional requirement for continuation in the office of President. In September 1992, the *Houston Post* railed at DeLay because he "ranked among the top congressional abusers of the free mailing privilege" by using taxpayer dollars for partisan political propaganda.

That didn't stop Tom DeLay, a few months later, from from running successfully for the leadership position of House Republican Conference Secretary and planning to jump over his "buddy" from Dallas, Dick Armey, and seek the number-two minority party whip spot when Bob Michel announced that he would resign, setting Gingrich's move up after the 1994 elections.

DeLay got his Republican whip job after the 1994 victory but it was not the number-two spot anymore. Unexpectedly Gingrich moved to Speaker of the House instead of minority party leader and Dick Armey kept his higher Texas pecking order by moving to Majority Leader of the House. Putting aside their competitiveness the two Texans buried the hatchet—in the anatomy of their common adversary, President Clinton, by leading the House in 1995 to a partisan display of intransigence which produced the government shutdown calculated to damage Clinton for the 1996 election.

DeLay flaunted his authority of the Republicans in the House in a famous burst of self-promotion when he said, "I'm very aggressive. I'm a hardworking, aggressive, persistent whip. That's why I'm whip." This trait was singled out for criticism in a conflict-of-interest corruption flap which the *Houston Chronicle*'s Washington Bureau disclosed in October 1995.

The *Chronicle* reported that Tom's younger brother, Randy DeLay, was the registered agent for the Mexican cement giant corporation CEMEX and was leading the charge in the House to kill a tariff which would give his client a good share of Texas's huge cement market. Randy was also the lobbyist for a group of highway interests while brother Tom served on the House Appropriation Committee's Subcommittee on Transportation.

House rules forbid members from proposing legislation or talking to federal agencies on matters in which they have a financial interest. The fact that DeLay's kid brother Randy had a big stake in the cement-highway issues put DeLay in jeopardy. Trying to stop trouble before it started, Randy put everyone "at ease" by stating that he was extremely sensitive to his brother's legal position and would not "cross the line" for his many big clients or for anybody else.

DeLay was not distracted by any such line. In his aggressive manner he co-signed letters on CEMEX's behalf and brazenly submitted an editorial page article to the *Houston Chronicle* defending Mexican companies that dumped their cement on the U.S. market, which could hardly be lost on the American highway builders who buy the cement. In September 1996 Ralph Nader announced that he had finally been allowed to file a complaint about DeLay with the Ethics Committee but the delay (no pun intended) he met made it unlikely that the complaint would even be considered before Congress adjourned for the elections to be held in November 1996.

In June 1997 DeLay announced that he had "banned" his brother Randy from lobbying his Washington offices. Tom's lawyer thought this was dispositive of the ethics charges and described the whip's move as answering to a "higher obligation" because banning Randy: "Now that's kind of important, because, I mean, it is his brother, and he wants to see him . . . and loves him."

The Ethics Committee has still not investigated the Nader charges nor the one that was made on 1998 national television by a sympathetic Clinton talking head who described the whip as "the bagman for the tobacco industry." This was a reference to DeLay's purported handing out of checks from his Leadership PAC, Americans for a Republican Majority (ARMPAC), which was funded by tobacco industry contributions to Republicans on the floor of the House.

The connection between the tobacco industry and DeLay's PAC is reported to be Ramhurst Corp., a small company located near the Winston-Salem, North Carolina, headquarters of RJR Nabisco. Ramhurst was started in 1993 with the support of RJR to combine "grassroots" lobbying among business groups and conservative activist organizations to quash federal efforts to regulate tobacco, and protect the tobacco companies from President Clinton's efforts to insulate children from the lure of smoking.

Significantly a key Ramhurst operative was chosen to head up DeLay's ARMPAC, a fundraising machine second only to Gingrich's in its successful accumulation of money. The connection works very well. By doling out impressive amounts to the Republican candidates for the house, DeLay has enormously increased his personal power and the organizational effectiveness of his whip in the Congress.

In July 1998 DeLay almost exceeded his 1996 Hypocrisy award when he rose in the House to condemn the fund-raising by the Democrats in 1996, suggesting that people whose names are hard to pronounce are likely to be foreigners and therefore their political contributions should be viewed with suspicion.

When one of his colleagues immediately urged DeLay to exclude Asians from his statement since his District has the largest concentration of Asians in all of Texas, DeLay quickly issued an apology to Asian-Americans and retracted his remarks.

A DeLay aide sought to excuse his bizarre stammering speech as a search for an inoffensive way to make his point about the Chinese connection to the Democrats. He said the whip was whipped by the lateness of the hour.

Indeed much of America is beginning to recognize how late the hour is for the passage of effective campaign finance reform legislation, especially in a seemingly uncooperative Republican-dominated Congress.

NEWT GINGRICH

King of the Hill

Newt Gingrich has a colorful family background according to a 1995 article in *Vanity Fair*. His grandfather was born out of wedlock and raised in a household in which his real mother posed as his sister. His father was a Navy man who left home after Newt was born and later allowed him to be adopted by his stepfather in exchange for not having to pay child support. Gingrich's mother said she is manic-depressive, and Newt's half-sister is an openly lesbian writer.

As a child, Gingrich told people that his goal was to become the Speaker of the House and he achieved it in record time—sixteen years after his first election in 1978. Newt Gingrich was born in Harrisburg, Pennsylvania on June 17, 1943 and came to Georgia to get his B.A. degree in 1965.

From there he earned a Master's Degree at Tulane University and went on for his Ph.D. degree in History in 1971. He returned to Georgia to teach at West Georgia College and embarked on his quest for the Speakership three years later, after losing his first two races for Congress in 1974 and 1976.

Although Gingrich grew up in a military environment, as the son of an Army officer, he personally saw no service since he was married with children during the Vietnam war. Newt's first marriage was to his high school math teacher. A former campaign worker, Anne Manning, told *Vanity Fair* in 1995 that she had a torrid affair with Gingrich while he was married to his first wife. In the same article, Manning called Gingrich morally dishonest, and said he had gone too far, and should be stopped before it's too late for America. Gingrich's first marriage is reported to have ended bitterly when he visited his wife's hospital room after her surgery for uterine cancer to discuss the terms of their divorce. He had to be pursued for adequate child support payments, although his book opines that any male who doesn't support his children is a bum.

In 1995 *Vanity Fair* reported that he spent far more time with Calista Bistek, a former congressional aide, and Arianna Huffington, who hosted a fifty-thousand-dollar-a-plate dinner for him, than with his second wife, Marianne, who had never actually moved to Washington and who has been candid about their marriage being "on and off." Gingrich once gave the marriage 53 to 47 odds of lasting.

His entry into Congress in 1978 did not begin auspiciously. He was disliked by the Democratic house leaders and hardly appreciated by Republicans in the Reagan and Bush White House. His meteoric rise in six years to Speaker and to a dominant role in American politics is all the more remarkable for that.

In 1987–1988 he orchestrated the ethics violations charges that brought down Democratic Speaker Jim Wright after Republican leaders in the House declined to make those charges. When it appeared in 1989 that he had succeeded in weakening Wright, who later resigned, back-bencher Gingrich ran against and beat the senior Edward Madigan for Republican whip, the number-two spot, by the one vote margin of eighty-seven to eighty-five in March 1989. Republican Minority leader Robert Michel decided not to get in Gingrich's way. He announced his retirement in 1993 and Gingrich effectively became the Republican leader in Congress a year before the 1994 elections.

By nationalizing his campaign with the Contract with America, signed by almost all the Republican candidates of the House, he was criticized as brash. But he surprised the pundits in the 1994 mid-term elections by picking up fifty-four seats. The Republican twenty-five-vote majority that was elected that year made Newt the surprise Speaker of the House and a contender for the Presidency. Party switches and special elections increased his margin to thirty-five votes before the 1996 elections.

When his own glass house was attacked by Democrats and some Republicans in 1996, Gingrich was shrewd enough to support Senator Bob Dole for President and bide his time. The Republican dominated Ethics Committee investigated secret donors to Newt's political action committee, and the prohibited use of charitable money to finance his political lecturing seminars in Georgia.

Gingrich's own ethics scandals are arguably more serious breaches of the public trust than lying about private sexual conduct. After he became Speaker of the House in 1995 he accepted a multimillion-dollar book advance from Harper-Collins, Rupert Murdoch's company, when Murdoch had legislation pending in Congress which substantially affected the Murdoch empire. The outcry forced Gingrich to repay the huge advance. He saved face by saying that the new contract would bring him much more in royalties from his book sales, a prediction which turned out to be woefully incorrect by more than half.

Gingrich was not a man of means before he became Speaker. He got into real trouble for accepting money from an exempt charitable foundation in return for teaching his political course on renewing America, and for not disclosing donors to his political action committee. As a result of these transgressions in January 1997, he signed a statement admitting his violations and agreeing to a rebuke from the House plus a stiff penalty of $300,000 to be paid within two years. Bob Dole, a registered lobbyist for Taiwan at the time, said he would lend Newt the money to pay the penalty but Gingrich announced five months before the deadline that he could pay the entire penalty without borrowing any money from Dole, a sum that apparently came from his book royalties.

Make no mistake about it, Newt Gingrich is the engine that will drive the House into voting impeachment charges against President Clinton, although he is politically savvy enough to know there is only a slight chance that he will be successful in removing Clinton from office.

In the Senate that would require sixty-seven votes for conviction. Both Newt Gingrich and Trent Lott know that they cannot expect that many votes once all the facts come out in the Congressional hearings and trial.

The politics and psychology of these men (there are few women in his cadre) make this agenda clear. Gingrich is using the inappropriate sexual conduct of Bill Clinton and Starr's perjury entrapment to achieve his first objective before the moderate Americans who swing close elections realize the hypocrisy of the Gingrich cadre, and what their victory might mean for America in the next century.

Gingrich sees himself as succeeding in his strategy because he is using the same tactics today that he has used in the past to vault himself over Republican leaders to his present position of power in the Congress.

After Dole lost to Clinton in 1997, Newt was able to make a deal in the face of these charges which allowed him to keep his job as Speaker. Gingrich signed a statement admitting ethical violations but blamed it on his failure to hire a lawyer. He accepted a reprimand and agreed to pay $300,000 as a penalty by January 1999.

What is happening today has to be seen in the context of what has been attempted before. Gingrich, after his unprecedented 1994 victory in the Congress, saw the 1996 Presidential election as the chance for the ideological supremacy of one party over the other. He hoped to be the one to lead that charge but he was stopped by his own party seniors, who believed a more moderate conservative could win. They used his personal trouble to encourage Gingrich to back off, where he bided his time, waiting for Dole's possible defeat to stage a comeback.

The slash and burn tactics that Newt Gingrich used against Jim Wright in 1987–1989 to attain the Congressional leadership of the Republican party are now being turned on Bill Clinton in 1997–1999 in order for Gingrich to attain the Presidency in 2000.

This seems to leave Newt in a vulnerable position. He has yet to admit the stories about his own prior marriage, that he did not remain faithful while his first wife was battling her cancer and that it was while she was in the hospital recovering from surgery, that he asked for a divorce to be free to marry again.

Newt has had little trouble raising campaign money since he became Speaker. Statistics released by the Federal Election Commission showed that in the 1994-96 election cycle Gingrich led the other four hundred thirty-four members of the House in fund-raising by a wide margin. His total of $6,252,000 was almost *twice* that of Democratic minority leader Richard Gephardt at $3,310,000.

There is little doubt that Gingrich will be re-elected in his Georgia congressional district and go on to preside over a crisis of historic magnitude. But that crisis will only be resolved by the people in the elections of 1998 and 2000, and not by the Congress. And that is precisely what Gingrich wants.

In that time, however, it will be interesting to see how Gingrich manages to uphold his image of a family values champion when the truth about his affairs, his divorcing of a cancer-stricken first wife and his ethics troubles become more widely known.

PHIL GRAMM

Taking Care of Things, Texas Style

O n the surface, the bespectacled, tall, long-necked Senator Phil Gramm of Texas looks like anything but a politician. A former University professor, Gramm looks like Mr. Peepers and sounds like a slow-talking molasses salesman.

In 1987, Gramm and his wife built a new home in Maryland. Gramm asked one of his campaign fund-raisers, Dallas S&L mogul Jerry Stiles, to build the house's interiors, including cabinets. At the time he was working for Gramm, Stiles was also under investigation by the FBI Dallas office for flagrant corruption.

Stiles agreed to build Gramm's interior for sixty-three thousand dollars. The work was done in Texas, then shipped to Maryland, along with Stiles's carpenters to assemble the interiors. The total bills came out to one hundred and seventeen thousand dollars, which was fifty-four thousand dollars over the original price.

However, Gramm only paid Stiles the originally agreed-upon price of sixty-three thousand dollars, and despite being stuck with a fifty-four-thousand-dollar tab, Stiles did not complain.

Critics and agents investigating the Stiles affair claimed that Stiles, *with Gramm's approval*, fraudulently inflated the bill to Gramm by nearly fifty percent, and then stole fifty-four thousand dollars from his S&L empire to put into his pocket to make up for the discrepancy in the Gramm bill. This allowed Gramm to get his new interior for sixty-three thousand dollars and provided Stiles with a mechanism for embezzling fifty-four thousand dollars from his own company.

FBI agents later investigated Stiles and found this fifty-four-thousand-dollar discrepancy very suspicious. According to one agent on the case, "Stiles is in this business for fifty years and he's going to be off by fifty percent? There's no doubt in my mind he knew what he was doing."

When Gramm learned the FBI was investigating his friend Stiles, he quickly paid Stiles the balance of fifty-four thousand dollars. But after the dust settled, Stiles secretly reimbursed Gramm the fifty-four thousand dollars.

Two years later, in 1989, Stiles's corrupt S&L empire collapsed, costing taxpayers an estimated $22 million. He was later convicted of eleven counts of conspiracy for fraud and is currently serving a fifty-five-year prison sentence in Texas.

But Stiles's friend, the senator from Texas, moved into his Maryland home and went on to run an (unsuccessful) campaign for President in 1996. He remains a champion of the right-to-lifers and Republican conservative crowd.

Gramm's wheeling-dealing with Stiles is reminiscent of another former Texas senator's machinations with swindlers Billie Sol Estes and Bobby Baker: Lyndon Johnson. Like Johnson, Gramm rolled along in his career while his cronies went to jail for criminal fraud.

Gramm appears to be a Republicanized version of the Johnsonian model of corruption for which Texas politics is notorious. Hopefully, he will also be able to display, in the matter that now faces the nation, the tremendous talent for statesmanship that also attends Texas politicians.

ALCEE HASTINGS

"Is There Life After Impeachment?"

Congressman Alcee Hastings of Florida has a unique distinction among the august members of Congress: he was actually impeached [as a federal judge] by Congress, yet only three years later went on to be elected to the very same Congress that had impeached him.

A firebrand orator, liberal political activist, and poor-man's-lawyer who had often represented clients for free, Hastings was the first black lawyer ever to be appointed as a federal judge in Florida. Federal judges, being appointed for life under the Constitution, can be removed from office only through impeachment by Congress and conviction by the Senate. Indeed, the process of impeaching a federal judge is quite similar to that of impeaching a U.S. President.

Hastings was nominated to the federal bench in December 1979, by then–President Jimmy Carter. He proudly perched upon the bench, like a great black eagle, and often blasted the Reagan administration from this vantage point for being racist and callous toward the poor and blacks. His outspoken attacks on the Republican president symbolized the politicization of the judiciary, and led to FBI investigations into Judge Hastings's role in allegedly accepting bribes from mob figures and embezzlers in exchange for handing down lenient sentences on them.

In 1989, the House actually impeached Hastings over charges of perjury, bribery and corruption, by a lopsided vote of 426–3, and sent the case to the Senate for a full trial.

On October 28, 1989, in the ornate and historical chamber of the U.S. Senate, no one smiled as ninety-five senators solemnly took their seats, a somber expression on their faces as they came to vote on whether the impeached judge should be convicted and removed from office.

Flanked by his lawyers and sitting behind a table in front of the Senate chamber, Judge Hastings glared intently at the senators who would decide his fate. The presiding officer, Senate majority leader Robert Boyd (Democrat, West Virginia) told the clerk to read the first impeachment charge—that Hastings had conspired with a crony to extort one hundred and fifty thousand dollars from two convicted embezzlers from Broward County, Florida, in exchange for reducing their sentences after their conviction on criminal charges.

After the clerk read the first charge of impeachment, Byrd looked out at the massive chamber and intoned, "Senators, how say you? Is the respondent, Alcee Hastings, guilty or not guilty?"

Conviction of an impeached federal judge, just like conviction of an impeached U.S. President, requires a vote of two-thirds of the senators present and voting. In this case, it would have required sixty-four of the ninety-five senators present.

After the roll call vote, Byrd read the results to the silent chamber: sixty-nine for impeachment, twenty-six for acquittal. Hastings was out of office, his career as a federal judge over. As the roll call dragged on with yet other charges against him, Hastings rose to his feet and strode defiantly out of the chamber. With his heels clicking across the marble floor, he walked to a pay phone, called his mother, and then strode outside to the throng of newsmen waiting at the foot of the Capitol steps.

Facing them, Hastings did not apologize, did not deny or admit anything. Instead, with the impeachment vote still ringing in his ears, he announced that he was going to go home and run for Governor of Florida. "My mama told me never to be afraid of the System," he said.

Hastings never did become governor, but three years later he ran as a candidate for Congress, seeking to become a member of the very body that had impeached him as a judge.

As of 1992, he had run unsuccessfully for eight offices in Florida, and now he was seeking his ninth office. Hastings was running for Congress from the newly created 23rd District, a heavily black-populated "Gold Coast" that ran from Palm Beach to Miami Beach. After the election votes were counted, to the astonishment of everyone, Hastings won the seat in Congress! "I don't think any real political professional gave him a chance," said Phil Hamersmith, a political consultant in Miami.

How had he pulled this off? According to Hamersmith, "among a certain population of black voters, Alcee Hastings was symbolic of someone who had fought the system, defied the Man." Hastings had run for Congress on an anti-Congress platform, charging the body he wished to join with racism and bigotry. In his campaign, he said that he had been unfairly impeached on essentially the same charges of bribery and obstruction of justice of which he had been acquitted in a criminal trial in 1983, six years earlier.

Since his impeachment in 1989, Hastings had become a powerful symbol of black frustration with the criminal justice system, and an exponent of the view that American justice was twisted, and often used to knock down black politicians who had risen too fast and too high.

Hastings reminded his audiences that as a black rebel trying to fight inside the system, he had always been—and always would be—a target. Even in his time at the predominantly African-American Howard University Law School, where he had been expelled for what the school called "non-seriousness of purpose," despite his B-average, Hastings claimed he had asserted independence by refusing to wear a suit and tie to class, and had been retaliated against via expulsion. After his expulsion, in a display of tenacity typical of Hastings, he struggled back and finished his legal education at Florida A&M University, where he got his J.D. in 1963.

After graduation, Hastings again defied the odds and the system by hanging out his own shingle in Fort Lauderdale, risking his career again and again in order to adhere to his principles, representing poor people for free, and fighting segregation in Florida's hotels and restaurants. He also volunteered his time as an unpaid counsel for the Fort Lauderdale NAACP.

After he became judge in 1979, Hastings was indicted on charges of taking a bribe. He acted as his own criminal defense attorney, and won an acquittal following a jury trial in 1984. Five years later in 1989 he was impeached by the House.

"Because he was black and outspoken, he broke the Rules of What Is Considered Respectable Behavior by a Judge," said a devoted supporter.

The Hastings Impeachment Investigation in Congress concluded that Hastings had misled jurors and fabricated evidence to get an acquittal in 1984. The Commission's five judges all recommended impeachment. The fourteen-judge Eleventh Circuit Court agreed, as did a twenty-six-member Judicial Committee of the U.S., which formally referred the Hastings case to Congress.

New, even uglier charges were leveled against Hastings as the impeachment inquiry ground on: he was accused of agreeing to take a million-dollar bribe from former Florida mob boss Santos Trafficante for fixing a case. He was accused of disgracing his judgeship by dealing with felons and criminals of all sorts, of being lenient with those who passed him money under the table.

Hastings, was then tried by a committee of twelve senators, led by Senator Arlen Specter (R-PA), a former prosecutor who initially castigated Hastings but later came to voice doubts about the strengths of the case for impeachment.

After his conviction in the Senate, Hastings not only ran for Congress but also appealed his conviction. In October 1992, just two weeks before his congressional election, Hastings was vindicated by U.S. Judge Stanley Sporkin, who ruled that the Senate trial had violated Hastings's constitutional rights because the Senate had held hearings only before the committee of Twelve, when in fact it should have held hearings before the entire Senate.

In a profession where ninety-nine percent is perception, Hastings was now perceived by voters as innocent and as the victim of a witch-hunt. The impeached, disgraced former judge now became a hero to the disenfranchised voters, who elected him to Congress and reelected him by wide margins in 1994 and 1996.

Hastings's roller-coaster career is an example of how little one's shortcomings seem to matter when there is no one to profit by them, and can best be summarized by one of his colleagues, who said during his 1992 campaign: "He's not running for sainthood—he's running for Congress."

ORRIN HATCH

Friends in High and
Low Places

Utah has been the most Republican state in five of the last six Presidential elections. In 1992, Perot got more votes there than Clinton. Its two Senators, Governor and three Representatives are all Republicans. Orrin Hatch, the sixty-four-year-old Senior Senator, is the leading public official in the state having served in the Senate since 1976 and will be up for his fifth term in 2000 unless he decides to seek the Presidency.

Hatch was born in Pittsburgh, Pennsylvania where he got his law degree, but attended college at Brigham Young University in Salt Lake City, where he now has his home.

Hatch grew up in Pittsburgh where his father was a metal worker. He practiced law there for a while before moving to Salt Lake City. At forty-two, he entered politics almost missing the dead-line for the Republican primary, which he won on the strength of an endorsement from Ronald Reagan. His real achievement was his upset of the eighteen-year incumbent Democrat, Frank Moss, in the general election.

In the Senate, Hatch has shown his strong conservative leanings. As a minority member of the Judiciary Committee, he defended the unsuccessful nomination of Robert Bork to the Supreme Court and was quite visible in the support of Justice Clarence Thomas in the Anita Hill hearings. He is a strong opponent of a woman's right to choose in abortion matters. In 1993, when the ninety-year-old Strom Thurmond left the ranking minority seat on the Judiciary Committee, Hatch took it and became Chairman when the Republicans won control in 1994.

Orrin Hatch will be in a key position if the House adopts impeachment charges before the new Congress takes their seats on January 3, 1999, which seems a real possibility. His public pronouncements during frequent appearances on the TV interview shows are that the Constitutional Process should go forward so that the Senate may consider the evidence.

His sympathies may be gleaned, however, from his defense of Kenneth Starr for "diversionary" attacks on Judge Starr's integrity and for his repeated attacks on Attorney General Janet Reno for not appointing an independent counsel to investigate Clinton's 1996 fund-raising practices.

Hatch got himself into trouble in 1993 when he was charged with trying to help a real estate developer get a loan from a Washington bank, BCCI, with foreign ownership that collapsed in a major scandal involving Clark Clifford, the long-time Democratic Adviser to Presidents who only escaped indictment because of his advanced age. Hatch defended BCCI on the Senate floor even after the bank pleaded guilty to charges of laundering drug money. Hatch's poll ratings dropped and, for a while, it appeared that he would have a close race for re-election in 1994, but the Senate Ethics Committee cleared him on all the BCCI charges before adjourning in 1993. He was then unopposed in the Republican primary and was re-elected with sixty-nine percent of the vote.

Hatch comes from a state which had to renounce polygamy before it obtained its statehood in 1896. The practice has not lost its attraction among women of Utah, as well as men, and there are communities there where the law prohibiting polygamy is not enforced. A few years ago, the author spent a pleasant week with the nine wives of the mayor of Big Water near the Arizona border.

All nine women thought their arrangement and their healthy, happy children, who were adopted by Mayor Alex Joseph, were the answer to the declining "family values" and divorce rates in America. Perhaps *this* is the solution our contry has been searching for in this age of moral decline.

Another unusual sexual lifestyle surfaced some years earlier in rumors about a woman on Hatch's staff with the screen name of Missy Manners, who starred in the X-rated movie "Behind the Green Door Part II." Missy Manners was reputed to be the exuberant daughter of wealthy Republican financial donors. After Senator Hatch dropped her from his staff, she went on to work in national Republican politics and was later heard to say that, during this period, she found that there was more sex going on in politics than in the pornographic film business.

If this story is true, then perhaps Hatch has seen enough to provide him with special credentials for his role in any Senate trial of the President's lifestyle.

KAY BAILEY HUTCHINSON

Senator Above the Law

In many ways, the changing political landscape of Texas has come to symbolize the changing political map of the United States as a whole: once solidly Democratic, the province of legendary politicians like LBJ and Sam Rayburn and John Connally, Texas switched over to the Republican camp in the 1970s and early 1980s.

And, whereas elected office had once been an all-male profession, women began to dominate it.

In 1992, Ann Richards became the first female governor of the Lone Star State.

Not far behind her was Kay Bailey Hutchinson, a rising star among Republican women. A former prom queen from LaMarque, Texas, Hutchinson had received her college and law degrees at the University of Texas. Graduating with J.D. in 1967, she was unable to find a job in law, and worked as a television reporter for Houston TV station KPRC.

She then moved to Dallas, got married, became the first woman elected to the Texas Legislature (1972), started her own candy business (McCraw Candies), got active in Republican politics and won an election as State Treasurer of Texas in 1990.

In June 1993, she ran in a special election for the U.S. Senate seat held by Lloyd Bentsen (who retired to take a cabinet post in the Clinton Administration).

She won the election against Bob Krueger, a naive Democratic politician who had been appointed by Governor Ann Richards to replace Bentsen temporarily, and who ran television commercials dressed in an Arnold Schwartzenegger "Terminator" costume.

Hutchinson won the runoff against Krueger by sixty-seven-percent to thirty-three-percent landslide, the largest margin in Texas in forty years.

But as soon as she took office in July 1993, Hutchinson found herself the target of a criminal investigation by Travis County liberal Democratic District Attorney Ronnie Earle, who brought criminal charges against her for allegedly using resources and employees in her state Treasurer's Office for campaign purposes, and for destroying documents by purging mailing lists of Texas voters from her computer.

In running for the Senate, Hutchinson was a protégé of Senator Bob Dole, the "Kingfish" of GOP sugar-daddy fundraising. Dole, who in 1993 became the dominant elected Republican politician in the country and who had the largest fundraising political machinery, personally hand-picked Hutchinson to run for the U.S. Senate in 1994. He showered her with campaign money from "Campaign America," his leadership PAC, and groomed her to be one of his myrmidons in his upcoming control of the Senate and his expected 1996 race for the presidency.

Hutchinson was accused of using her State Treasurer Office as a de facto campaign headquarters, using millions of dollars of taxpayer money and resources and staff to perform illegal campaign functions and for destroying evidence in her computer by purging mailing lists of voters and campaign contributors, and she was formally arrested and charged for these crimes shortly after taking office as U.S. Senator in the summer of 1993.

Hutchinson immediately accused the Democratic D.A. of staging a bogus criminal prosecution against her, but the case went forward. As a freshman U.S. Senator, she found herself totally diverted from business at hand, had to shuttle between Travis County and Washington, and hired an army of lawyers and P.R. specialists, as she prepared for an embarrassing criminal trial.

While it is illegal under Texas state criminal law (and under federal law and most states' laws) to use a state government office and staff for federal campaign purposes, this practice is far more common than is generally acknowledged. Indeed, as the author observed when he worked for Dole, Dole himself used to do this all the time, using his staff to shake lobbyists for money while they asked for the Senator's vote on bills, and using the staff to campaign for the candidate.

What is rare is to see an actual criminal prosecution for this common conduct. Most prosecutors in the country, and especially in Texas, would look the other way when told about such conduct, because they know that "every politicians does this."

What is unusual about the Hutchinson situation, according to the prosecutors, is the extent and brazenness with which she used her State Treasurer's office staff to run her U.S. Senate campaign.

According to witnesses and documents subpoenaed by the Travis County D.A., Hutchinson personally directed her staff to make phone calls, raise money, attend campaign functions and prepare her speeches as she ran for U.S. Senate—all at Texas state taxpayer expense.

The D.A. refused to drop the case despite pressure from Dole and others, and the case was set to go to trial in February 1994, when the D.A. suddenly and mysteriously dismissed the entire case before the judge ruled on the admissibility of evidence seized by the police in a June 1993 raid into the State Treasurer Office in Austin.

The official reason given by Ronnie Earle for the dismissal was that the law enforcement authorities had obtained documents against Hutchinson by an illegal search-and-seizure operation which violated Hutchinson's Fourth Amendment Rights (so she claimed), without a proper search warrant, from Hutchinson's old State Treasurer office. But this seems like a lame excuse for dropping the case, since the D.A. had known all along about the validity of the search warrant, and had insisted for years that the search had been perfectly legal. Also, the D.A. had live witnesses prepared to testify against Hutchinson, that she had bullied and forced them to work on her campaign for Senate, while they were on the state Treasurer's payroll. One witness, daughter of former Texas Governor John Connally, even was prepared to testify that Hutchinson had physically assaulted her in this ugly mess.

It is also interesting to note that although Hutchinson herself saved her neck by invoking the Fourth Amendment, in the Senate world of legislating, she has consistently supported harsh criminal laws which would do away with Fourth Amendment protections against warrantless searches and seizures by the police against ordinary citizens. She has been a professed "law and order" champion who may have violated the law herself, and gotten away with it.

It would seem that the real reason why Hutchinson got off the hook may be quite different. As we have seen with so many other demigods of Congress, once you get into Congress, you are above the law. At least, there is an expectation that you are above the law, that law enforcement authorities don't mess with you, and that you can get away with anything.

It is, perhaps, this hubris which leads so many congresspersons and senators into flirting with dangerous, compromising situations that sometimes result in scandals.

As with Senator Ted Kennedy's inquest over Chappaquidick, Senator Carol Moseley-Braun's alleged criminal conduct, and Congressman Floyd Flake's indictment and other matters, it seems that people put on a magical cloak of immunity from ordinary criminal law when they enter the hallowed grounds of Congress. Senator Hutchinson was quite a different defendant than Citizen Hutchinson. Like her congressional colleagues, she seems to be "above the law."

Hutchinson's bout with the criminal law did not affect her standing much with the voters. In November 1995, Texas voters sent her back to the Senate with a sixty-one-to-thirty-eight percent victory as she won a full six-year term in that august body.

While Hutchinson now argues that Clinton should be impeached because he is "not above the law," it would seem that in her own controversial criminal case of illegal campaign activities, her status as U.S. Senator put her "above the law."

JAY KIM

The Convicted Congressman in an Ankle Bracelet

The 41st Congressional District of California is perched on the eastern end of the Los Angeles Basin, called the Inland Empire, where Los Angeles and Orange and San Bernardino counties come together. Originally a lush agricultural area of orange and lemon groves during Southern California's pristine heyday, the area is now largely industrialized and dominated by fast-growing, fast-moving corporations specializing in highway building and the like.

Congressman Jay Kim, a Korean-American, was a former city engineer, mayor and owner of a construction conglomerate, Jaykim Engineers, which designed highways, water reclamation plants and other large projects financed mostly by government money.

A conservative Republican, he easily won a House seat in 1992 in a solidly Republican district that voted for Bush over Clinton by a wide margin.

But Kim's honeymoon in Congress was short-lived. After just six months in office, in July 1993, Kim was pounded by the *Los Angeles Times,* which reported that Kim's own company spent four hundred thousand dollars on his campaign, an illegal corporate contribution (since 1907, federal law has banned corporations from contributing any money directly to any federal campaign for congress). Kim claimed somewhat unconvincingly that three hundred thousand dollars of this money was a personal salary to him, but had difficulty explaining why he had not paid the company any rent for use of its office space or otherwise acted as a salaried employee of the company.

Kim went on to win re-election in 1994. But in late 1995 and early 1996, more scandal erupted: It was revealed that five prominent South Korean Companies, including Korean Air Lines, Hyundai, and Samsung, had made corporate and foreign contributions to Kim's campaigns, contributions that were in violation of federal law. The five companies all pled guilty to criminal charges and paid a total of $1.6 million in fines. They admitted to having illegally reimbursed their own employees for making bogus "conduit straw man" contributions to Kim's 1992 campaign. Kim denied knowledge of these illegalities.

In addition, the FBI investigated several additional charges involving Kim and illegal money being funneled into his 1992 campaign.

Not surprisingly Kim's 1996 primary opponent, Bob Kerns, accused Kim of "a pattern of dishonesty and lack of integrity."

At the time Kim countered by claiming victimhood: "Number one: I am a Republican, and nine out of ten reporters are registered Democrats," he charged. "Number two: I am an Asian. And some media people just don't like to see a conservative Asian American." Like Alcee Hastings, Kim has been able to exploit his racial minority status to pose as a victim of white racism, thereby obfuscating his culpability, whenever anyone accused him of high crimes and misdemeanors.

In 1996, Kim won a shaky victory against Kerns, a rabid Pat Buchanan apostle, who ran ads subtly hinting that Kim was a dishonest Asian. Kerns's theme song was: "Truth and Integrity. The American Way." But Kim, far better financed than the Buchananite, won by fifty-eight to forty-two percent in the primary, and went on to win the general election by fifty-eight to thirty-three percent.

But to make matters worse, in April 1997, Kim's 1994 campaign treasurer, another Korean named Seokuk Ma, was convicted of criminally concealing illegal campaign contributions to Kim's campaign. Kim himself was indicted in early 1998 and pled guilty in court to accepting more than two hundred and fifty thousand dollars in illegal campaign contributions in 1992, taking fifty thousand dollars from a Taiwanese national, taking twelve thousand dollars from a New York corporation, and failing to report eighty-three thousand dollars in services provided to his campaign by an engineering firm he owned. He was even forced to wear an electronic ankle bracelet under his pants while serving in Congress, and was restricted by the sentencing judge to going only from his apartment to Capitol Hill for work. He was also sentenced to two hundred hours of community service and fined five thousand dollars.

Like Hastings, Kim is a case which nobody in Congress wanted to touch—a tar baby that will tarnish anyone with the label "racist" for criticizing Kim, and "crook" for supporting him. In the increasingly polarized mode of U.S. politics, Kim had become a sort of disreputable uncle no one wants to get too close to.

"It's like an awkward family dinner," said one

Republican congressman of the elusive Kim. "You just don't talk about it."

Kim has since become a kind of pariah, restricted to his Congressional office and Fairfax home, left alone and kept at a distance.

"It's an awkward situation for everyone," said Congressman David Dreier (R–Calif).

Even Democrats have been strangely silent when it comes to Kim. "We think he's more of a liability if they [the Republicans] continue to allow him to be an active player in the party," commented one Democrat activist.

Convicted and wearing an electronic ankle bracelet under his suit pants, enabling federal probation officials to track his movements, Kim was restricted to his Capitol Hill office and his apartment seventeen miles away in suburban Fairfax, Virginia. There, Kim quietly went about his business, voting conservative Republican at every opportunity. Brazenly, he asked the sentencing judge to "stay" his sentence until after the June primary in California, so that he could campaign at home. The judge denied the stay, thus forcing Kim to remain within the seventeen-mile radius of Washington, and requiring him to dispatch an army of surrogates to campaign for him in California.

The spectacle of having a convicted criminal

serving in Congress instead of going to jail, and running for re-election by remote control while wearing an ankle bracelet, fully justified the joke that "Kim has turned the House of Representatives into the House of Corrections."

The fact that Kim was not expelled from Congress, despite his conviction, is a testimony to the ethics of those who ably served with him in the "House of Corrections."

Kim is actually only the third House member in congressional history to have retained his seat in Congress after being convicted of a crime. His two illustrious predecessors performed this feat in 1798 and 1956.

According to the U.S. Attorney's office in Los Angeles, Kim admitted to committing the "largest amount of campaign violations in history by a member of Congress." More than thirty-three percent of the contributions to his 1992 campaign, where he eked out a win by a mere eight hundred and eighty-nine votes, were admitted by Kim in 1998 to have been illegal.

"Jay Kim probably stole a congressional election in 1992 by this fraudulent campaign financing scheme," says Gary Ruskin, director of the congressional watchdog group, Congressional Accountability project. "In my view, Jay Kim's presence cheapens the moral authority of every other member there."

Barred by his criminal sentence from even traveling home to his California district, Kim was still determined to seek reelection in 1998.

Kim's estranged wife of thirty-six years, June Kim, has sued for divorce and turned against her husband, assisting the House Ethics Committee in investigating him for corruption. "He is a congressman. He should be clean. He should be a role model," said June, who also pled guilty to accepting illegal campaign donations. "In fact," she added, "he is the most crime-committing person I know."

June was amazed that her husband was still in Congress, despite pleading guilty to major crimes. "It's really frustrating that our law is not tough enough to get him out right away," she noted. "He's humiliated us enough." She added that Kim was guilty of an even wider conspiracy to violate congressional campaign financing laws, and of lying under oath and deceiving the Ethics Committee investigating him.

Yet California Republican congressmen, such as Jerry Lewis, arrogantly continued to predict that Kim, running his campaign from 3,000 miles away, out of his one bedroom apartment in Fairfax, would defy the odds and remain in office. "Jay," said Lewis, "I expect, will be with us for a long time." Lewis was wrong, but only by a hair.

While Kim has made history by turning the House of Representatives into a "House of Corrections," it is significant that until he pled guilty to the crimes in court, his colleagues in the House had not seriously moved to expel or even censure him for flagrant violation of the campaign financing laws. "If we did that, we would disenfranchise his constituents," said a Republican colleague.

He hired a lawyer from Johnnie Cochran's firm to represent him when the House Ethics Committee finally mounted a major press against him in early 1998, threatening to expand its scope to investigate his questionable campaign practices not only for 1992, but for 1994 and 1996 as well.

Finally, in the June 1998 primary, Kim was defeated in his bid for a fourth term in Congress. But really, not a bad run for a man who seemed to embody so obviously Mark Twain's aphorism about criminals and Congress.

DENNIS KUCINICH
Flair, Zest and a Love of Labor

Dennis Kucinich was elected to the Cleveland City Council when he was twenty-three and was a one-term mayor there at thirty-one. Never really leaving his love for politics, he spent the next eighteen years maturing as a radio talk-show host, lecturer, consultant and TV reporter. In 1996 he saw a chance to unseat the incumbent Republican Martin Hoke who had been elected twice in the west side of Cleveland and the western suburbs of Cuyahoga County, Ohio's 10th District.

Hoke was vulnerable. He had purchased $50,000 in GTE stock before voting on a tele-communications bill in the House. Hoke also had an eye, and perhaps more, for women's anatomy. He had been caught in an embarrassing moment of vulgarity in 1994. Clinton was giving his State of the Union message in the House chamber. Hoke was being set up with a TV mike to give a Republican reaction to the TV audience. A shapely woman TV producer, Lisa Dwyer, was wiring the mike to a leering Hoke. He turned to a fellow member of the Ohio congressional delegation and said, into the microphone which Hoke did not know was already activated, "She has bi-i-i-g breasts."

Kucinich won by a slim 6,200 votes despite his opponent's campaign charge that he accepted a $5,000 contribution from the Laborers Union which had links to the mob. No problem. Kucinich is single and can, with impunity, admit to lust, in his heart and elsewhere. It's just not hokey for him to emulate Hoke. His race for the golden Cleveland spot in Congress was a torrid one. He had to defend his questionable ties to particular labor groups. With his TV flair for publicity, a zest for confrontation and a tenacity that is his trademark, he said about those ties: "Are they my special interest? Yes . . . I am not a missionary for labor; I am for the house of labor, the family of labor."

Kucinich made a clean breast of his special interest, denying any missionary position in favor of the family. It was good enough to win a close race, but will it be enough in the 1998 race for the gold?

BOB LIVINGSTON
No Stranger to Entrapment

Robert L. (Bob) Livingston was elected to Congress from the 1st District of Louisiana in a 1977 special election, after the incumbent was forced to resign for the fraud which later sent him to jail. Livingston went to Congress with that background, and was very tough on his House colleagues while on the Ethics Committee during the Abscam investigation.

Abscam is short for the FBI's sting in using a phony Arab sheikh to catch selected members of Congress in using their influence in exchange for money. The scam was run by law enforcement officials to catch the legislators in the act with hidden video cameras. Reputations were trashed. Indictments and convictions followed. There was a public glee over the pictures on TV, and no outcry over trapping corrupt public officials, but the backlash, when it came, was over prosecutorial emtrapment. Questions were raised about selecting an official who was not seeking a bribe, and using an undercover FBI agent to criminalize him because you suspect that he could be bribed.

The FBI Abscam "sting" in 1980 caught New Jersey Senator Harrison Williams on tape, saying how he could get a lucrative government contract in return for valuable stock. Six House members were caught. Republican Richard Kelly of Florida was seen stuffing $25,000 in bills into his pants and wondering aloud, "Does it show." Republican Senator Larry Pressler of South Dakota was set up for the Abscam sting during his first term in the Senate. He was clean, naive or smart enough to tell the FBI agent in Arab headdress, "Wait a minute. What you are suggesting may be illegal." He was the only one to escape entrapment. He was re-elected twice to his Senate seat, before losing in a nasty contest in which a columnist, without offering evidence, accused him of being gay.

Bob Livingston is a lawyer. He was a prosecutor in the United States Attorney's office. He approaches politics with a prosecutorial, aggressive, right-wing conservative frame of mind. He owns alligator-skinning knives known in the Big Easy as a "Cajun Scalpel," and he brought one along once to a Congressional committee meeting. Livingston has exhibited little unhappiness at the thought of skinning the President.

He is also a power in the House. In 1995, Gingrich knighted Livingston to be the powerful chairman of the Appropriations Committee, shunting aside Representative Joseph McDade (R-PA) who had been indicted in 1992 for financial corruption in office. This took some arm-twisting by Newt because at the time House Republicans (unlike Democrats) did not require indicted members to resign from top committee assignments and McDade coveted the Appropriations chair. It didn't prove to be cause for lasting concern.

When McDade's indictment finally went to trial in 1996, the trail was cold, witnesses were dead and the memories of others faded. The presumption of innocence prevailed, a not guilty verdict was delivered and McDade tried to reclaim the Appropriations chair. The powerful Livingston, with Newt's help, mollified McDade with the offer of the Vice Chairmanship of Appropriation.

As Kurt Vonnegut might say: "So it goes."

Bob Livingston, like others of his political persuasion, got caught up in the Iran-Contra affair and evidence surfaced that he had attended a meeting on March 4, 1985 with the later-indicted National Security Adviser Robert McFarlane, where it appeared that Livingston was caught by that Watergate mantra, "What did he know and when did he know it." The *when* was clear—it *was* when the illegal funneling of hot funds to the Contras was in its ascendancy. The *what* was within a narrow rim of deniability but the thrust of the written notes of the meeting is that Livingston was told by McFarlane what he was doing. The "Prosecutor in Congress" escaped prosecution. So it goes.

TRENT LOTT

The Man from Pascagoula is in Charge

Everyone in America with a TV set has seen the Junior Senator from Mississippi who was elected the Republican Majority Leader of the United States Senate after serving there for only eight years, beating even Lyndon Johnson's record for the Meteoric Rise Award. His dominant role in any Senate impeachment trial, if the House votes the charges against Bill Clinton, has ignited broad public interest in his regular appearances on network news shows and C-SPAN.

Lott grew up in Pascagoula, Mississippi, the son of a shipyard pipefitter and a teacher. He still makes his home there, which is the site of Ingalls Shipbuilding, a unit of Litton Industries, and the largest private employer in Mississippi with eleven thousand workers at its eight-hundred-acre yard.

Lott went to Ole Miss, receiving his Bachelor's and Law degrees in 1963 and 1967. He practiced law for about a year before he took a job with Democratic Congressman William Colmer. When Colmer retired in 1972, Lott, at thirty, obtained Colmer's endorsement and won the House seat— as a Republican.

In 1974, Trent Lott was the youngest member of the House Judiciary Committee and said that Nixon's conduct did not rise to the level of impeachable offenses, a remarkably different view than he now expresses about Bill Clinton. Lott came up the party hierarchy in the House with the same speed he later exhibited in the Senate. By 1980, he was in the number-two spot as the Republican whip. In 1988 he chose to give up the chance of becoming Speaker of the House in order to run for the Senate.

In 1994 Lott bypassed his colleague, the Senior Senator from Mississippi, the number-three party leader, Thad Cochran, when he challenged moderate Alan Simpson for whip and won by a single vote. Asked about Cochran, Lott said, "There comes a time in politics, as in baseball, when you seize the moment or it's gone forever. I ran and he didn't."

In 1996, when Majority Leader Bob Dole resigned from the Senate to give full attention to his run for the Presidency, Cochran did seize the moment to challenge his junior Mississippi friend but was too late and Lott won by the wide margin of forty-four to eight. He said, "The torch has been passed, but the flame is the same."

Pretty soon, however, it became clear on the central political issue facing the nation that the flame was not the same, but was blazing in arrogant deference to prevent a vote on campaign finance reform even though the McCain-Feingold bill enjoyed majority support in 1997 and 1998. In fact, Lott's Senate has been one of the least productive in modern history, leading Democrats to call the 105th Congress "The Do-Nothing Congress."

In June 1998, Lott got legislation started for a new $1.5 billion helicopter carrier the Navy had not even requested because it will surely be built in Pascagoula. He added to the military authorization and appropriations bills a $50 million purchase of parts for the carrier. The Navy had seven helicopter carriers in service or under construction and all of them were built by Ingalls. When Ingalls' executives come to Washington to talk about a healthy backlog to keep full employment in his hometown, Lott's top aides do not have to be told to listen up.

One lobbyist who knows the heft of Lott's influence said, "This is the type of thing that Majority Leaders do."

Lott is understandably an outspoken supporter of aggressive defense spending. In late 1996 he succeeded in getting the Navy to agree to build six new destroyers at Ingalls, beginning in 1998, and then succeeded in moving up the time for the construction of two additional destroyers for which contracts would not have been given out for at least five years.

Trent Lott is *the obstacle* to changing the way elections are financed in America. After a private luncheon in February 1997 with two hundred of his party's most generous financial backers, he was asked whether the luncheon gives the impression that rich people can buy access to Congress. His answer explains why campaign finance reform is still bottled up in the Senate: "I support people being involved in the political process. We're not for food stamps for politicians; we don't think public financing of campaigns is a good idea."

The luncheon guests had each given at least $175,000 over four years to the Republican National Committee. They were part of the so-called Team 100, not because there are only one hundred of them, but so named because the entry fee is $100,000. Lott said that letting big money donors have the opportunity to contribute such large sums is "the American Way."

The American Way was in clear view when

Congress raised the minimum wage to $5.15 per hour in 1996. By setting the floor for big business to pay at least $206 for a forty-hour week, the Republicans tacked on a few provisions that had nothing to do with minimum wages, but added up to $21 billion in handouts to special interests of corporate America. That law allowed Wall Street buyout moguls to deduct fees to banks and advisers from their income taxes, canceled a surtax on diesel fuel for luxury cars and yachts, allowed seafood processors in Senator Murkowski's State of Alaska to deduct the cost of workers' meals, and permitted newspapers to treat individual distributors as independent contractors rather than employees for whom they would have to pay social security taxes.

At a time when his party was criticizing Clinton, Gore and the Democrats for campaign finance irregularities, which would be corrected by the bill, he gave a phony reason for refusing to allow a Senate vote. He said that there was a "constitutional right" for corporations, rich individuals and labor unions to feed the political system with huge campaign donations. At the same time he proposed an amendment to limit the ability only of labor unions to spend money in politics because they are traditional Democratic supporters.

Trent Lott exhibits the charm of his native state;

he is gregarious, personable and on good terms with the other senators whose support he needs. He will not easily yield a level playing field to the opposition party nor change the financing of national elections to reduce the influence of big money interests. As we've seen before, this is an issue that is far more ominous than sexual impropriety, yet is too complex to be communicated easily to the voters.

JOHN MCCAIN

American Hero Tarnished by Association

John McCain is the Senior Senator from Arizona first elected in 1986 and now seeking his third term in the Senate. He is one of the more respected senators, admired by Democratic and Republican senators alike, and is considered a possible candidate for President in 2000. His record on most issues is conservative but there are some unusual departures which may make him tough to beat in the Republican primaries in the Spring of 2000.

McCain was born August 29, 1936 and is a 1958 graduate of the United States Naval Academy where he was known as both a fearless leader and a hell-raiser. He became a pilot and earned a reputation as a carouser and ladies' man, which should not hurt his chances to become President.

As President Cleveland said when he was elected despite the charges of fathering an illegitimate child, "The American people do not want a gelding in the White House."

McCain's heroism is not yet well known in the country. He sought an assignment to fly his Skyhawk fighter in Vietnam and was decorated in action. In October 1967, his plane was downed by a SAM missile but he survived with a broken leg and two broken arms.

McCain's personal story is a dramatic one, told by Robert Timberg in *The Nightingale's Song.* He is the son and grandson of Navy admirals and his father was Commander in Chief of all United States Forces in the Pacific when McCain was a prisoner in Vietnam. He spent five years in Communist war camps, most of the time in pain, torture and starvation. Yet he refused to be released before other prisoners who had been there longer when he was offered to be let out because of his father's rank and the propaganda advantage that would give the enemy. McCain returned to the United States in March 1973 and in 1980 moved to Arizona which was the home state of his wife, Cindy Lou. When he ran for the Senate in 1982 and was attacked as an outsider, he said, "The longest place I ever lived in was Hanoi."

The story of McCain and what came to be

known as "The Keating Five" is an example of how one slip of judgment, even to accommodate Senate colleagues, can become a nightmare of hard-ball politics. Nothing could be more illustrative of President Harry Truman's advice that "If you can't take the heat, stay out of the kitchen" than how McCain took the heat of the Keating Investigation and bounced back to be a contender for that kitchen. McCain and Senator John Glenn, the astronaut hero who is retiring from the Senate this year to take another trip into space, were eventually cleared by the Senate Ethics Committee after a two-year investigation. John McCain said that the Keating experience caused him more pain than he had known during his worst days as a prisoner in Vietnam.

The Keating story, however, is a stark example of how senators and representatives use their influence to protect and assist big contributors for money. McCain's lapse of judgment in getting involved with the three senators who were over the ethical line on campaign contributions may explain his present crusade to clean up the disgraceful state of how many incumbents get their money for reelection.

Charles Keating is said to resemble a tall mortician. He became well known in the 1970s as a crusader against pornography and drugs. In 1979 when the Securities and Exchange Commission accused him of defrauding stockholders of a Cincinnati based Savings & Loan by approving $14 million of preferential loans to himself and other company insiders, he agreed to a consent judgment and a big fine.

In 1984 Keating went to California and bought Lincoln Savings & Loan in Irvine for $50 million. He soon engaged in a flurry of questionable business practices which federal bank regulators regarded as illegal. Ed Gray was the Chairman of the Federal Home Loan Bank Board which regulated S & Ls. In March 1986, his San Francisco office began an investigation of Keating and Lincoln.

Keating eventually went to prison, but in 1986–87 he was a successful businessman with major interests in California, Michigan, Arizona and Ohio who had given five senators from those states more than a million dollars for their campaigns. He involved the five senators in trying to intimidate Ed Gray and the federal regulators who were struggling to expose Keating's crimes.

One of Keating's allies was Alan Cranston, the former senator from California who once said, "A person who makes a contribution has a better chance to get access than someone who does not." When reporters asked Keating if his donations had bought personal favors, replied, "I certainly hope so." In March 1987, Keating's Lincoln S & L contributed one hundred thousand to a Senator Cranston project. A month later in April 1987, Cranton attended two meetings with Ed Gray and his federal regulators at which time he tried to intimidate them into being lenient with Keating. In addition to Cranston, Keating had made substantial contributions to Dennis DeConcini and Donald Riegle, former senators from Arizona and Michigan. At Keating's request they actively defended Lincoln S & L from supposedly unfair treatment by the bank board regulators in 1987.

At the April 9, 1987 meeting with the regulators in San Francisco, DeConcini told them that the five senators were meeting with them because their actions could injure a constituent and De-Cocini suggested that a bank rule not be enforced against Lincoln. The regulators told the senators that Keating was involved in a whole range of actions for which they were sending a criminal referral to the Department of Justice. While Senators McCain and Glenn broke off any further efforts to assist Keating, DeConcini, Cranston and Riegle's behavior was different. They continued to help Keating and accepted his money for their campaigns.

The Lincoln S & L disaster that ultimately followed was one of the largest bankruptcies in the ensuing scandal. By 1989 the entire country was waking up to the fact that they had been robbed of literally hundreds and hundreds of billions of dollars. In October 1989, the Senate finally took notice and its Ethics Committee undertook an investigation to determine whether the senators' actions violated the federal election laws or the Senate's Rules of Conduct.

The Ethics Committee consisted of six senators. Three were Republicans: Jesse Helms and Trent Lott who are top leaders today in the Senate, and Warren Rudman, the former senator who retired in 1992 and later wrote about the "Keating Five" in his 1996 book *Combat*. The three Democrats were Howell Heflin, Terry Sanford and David Pryor, all of whom have left the Senate.

The investigation ran on for two years. In another one of the frequent reappearances of lawyers in Washington, Bob Bennett, who was later to be Clinton's lawyer in the Paula Jones case, was counsel to the Ethics Committee in the Keating Five Investigation. Despite Bennett's efforts for stronger action, what finally happened is a prime example of the unwillingness of the Senate to discipline even the most obvious unethical behavior.

The Committee's action never went to a floor vote in the Senate. Even Senator Cranston, the worst offender, received only a reprimand from the Committee, which was filed with the clerk of the Senate and presented on the Senate floor without debate or a vote. Senator Riegle received a milder criticism, simply a rebuke because his conduct gave the appearance of being improper. Senator DeConcini also received a rebuke with the Committee saying that his aggressive conduct with the regulators was inappropriate. The actions against Senators McCain and Glenn were dismissed because the Committee concluded that they had simply exercised poor judgment in meeting with the regulators and such a lapse did not call for disciplinary action.

Several conclusions can be drawn from this case today. Four of the six senators who served on the Ethics Committee left the Senate. We believe their experience on the Committee, not only with the five senators being investigated but with the process of the Committee, was a factor in their leaving public service. Of course the other two members, Majority leader Trent Lott and Jesse Helms, the Chairman of the Foreign Relations Committee, remain.

What has McCain learned from all this association with crooks and collaborators? Well, he is out in front on the Senate's efforts to enact meaningful campaign finance reform. McCain would eliminate political action committees and soft money, ban gifts from lobbyists, and give candidates some free television time and lower television ads and postage rates in return for voluntary spending limits. In 1996 McCain and Democratic Senator Russ Feingold of Wisconsin sponsored such a bill. It was endorsed by President Clinton who is still facing charges of illegal fund-raising. McCain favors an independent counsel to investigate those charges against the President.

The Republican leadership has blocked the McCain–Feingold bill from going to the floor of the Senate where there appears to be enough Democratic and Republican votes to pass it. The irony of the Republican Party standing in the way of changing the money game in politics while launching Congressional investigations of how the Democrats, not the Republicans, played that game in 1996 has not been lost on the media or the public. McCain's straightforward position *against* abuses in the present campaign finance law and for changing it to reduce the money advantage of incumbents may make him a strong contender in 2000.

So though McCain may have leaned from his experience, others did not. Or at least, they didn't learn the same lesson. Lott and Helms can be seen frequently on television saying how the Senate must continue the impeachment process and warning the President about trying to have his Democratic supporters prevent a public trial on the Senate floor. Several hundred billion dollars of the public's money was stolen in the S & L scandal and they did not even speak out in the Committee report for censure. President Clinton had an inappropriate consensual sexual relationship and sought to keep it private. For this conduct, Lott and Helms are unwilling to consider censure or a public rebuke and are insisting on a circus trial in hopes of exacting extreme punishment. Is that hypocrisy or integrity? Are they the honored statesmen they purport to be?

The answer belongs to the American people. The Keating Three, who were called to mild account by the Committee, were never again elected to public office by the people. The final judgment of Clinton's conduct also belongs to the people. Should Trent Lott or Jesse Helms have the desire to stand for national office, the people will have to decide whether they acted out of integrity or hypocrisy.

JOHN MICA

How You're Gonna Keep Him Down in Orlando After He's Seen Parie

John Mica is the Congressman from the safe Republican 7th District of Florida which includes Daytona and part of Orlando. Mica lists his assets as well above $2.25 million. He has homes in Winter Park, Florida, near Rollins College, as well as in Washington and North Carolina. He has said about his job: "I've made a lot of money. I don't need the salary and I don't need the title."

However, when he took his wife Patricia to Paris for ten days after he was re-elected in 1996, the cost was paid for by ISTED, a French company that wants to bring high-speed rail to Florida. Mica sits on the Surface Transportation Subcommittee of the House Transportation and Infrastructure Committee.

Mica made his fortune in business, in one case

turning 360 feet of New Smyrna beachfront in his district into profitable real estate. He understands how business interests use money to influence Congress. Before crossing over, Mica was himself a lobbyist representing American Specialty Chemical. His Republican opponent in the 1992 primary for Congress criticized his representation of special interests rather than the interests of Florida or the United States. Mica won that race in 1992 and has been in Congress ever since.

He disdains welfare recipients whom he describes as alligators. In the 1995 welfare reform debate, he used his broad brush to say, "If left in their natural state, alligators can take care of themselves."

In 1997, besides his junket to France, Mica took trips to Cooperstown, N.Y., Mount Pocono, PA, and St. Louis, none of which made a ripple in his millions, the salary he said he doesn't need, or the $500,000 given to him by the government to run his offices. All that travel was paid for by businesses and other private interests. Obviously Mica can take care of himself, too.

CAROL MOSELEY-BRAUN

The Sword and the Shield in the Land of Lincoln

Senator Carol Moseley-Braun has an enviable distinction: the first African-American woman ever elected to the U.S. Senate (in 1992), and the only black senator now in office. She hails from the legendary Land of Lincoln and has been the only black senator during her six years in office.

A native Chicagoan and graduate of the prestigious University of Chicago Law School (JD, 1972), Moseley-Braun became a federal prosector right out of law school, was elected to the Illinois Legislature in 1978, became Assistant Majority Leader in 1983 and went on to become Cook County (Chicago) Recorder of Deeds from 1989 to 1992.

She has been accused of being a modern-day, slick, African-American version of the old corrupt

Daley Machine that ran Chicago ("Crook County") for so many decades.

Moseley-Braun is perhaps the most self-destructive member of the Senate, with a passion for foot-in-mouth disease and a seemingly broad ethical blindspot. Instead of earning kudos for her performance as the first black female in the Senate, Moseley-Braun has developed a reputation for sleazy misconduct, and has been accused of using her race as a shield and a sword, to ward off her accusers.

Her election in 1992 to the Senate was itself a fluke, as she surprised everyone by upsetting Alan Dixon, the veteran Democratic incumbent with forty years in elected office.

As early as September 1992, when she was still running for the Senate (she ran under the surname "Braun" and added the "Moseley-" in 1993), she was accused of dishonesty when it was revealed that three years earlier, she had split among herself and her three siblings a $28,750 timber royalty inheritance owed to her mother, who was then a nursing home resident living off Medicaid, and who was legally obligated to reimburse Medicaid for this money.

Moseley-Braun failed to offer any credible explanation for this seeming illegality (many people across the country are prosecuted every day for Medicaid fraud in situations similar to this, but Moseley-Braun was untouched by politically astute prosecutors), and she won the November 1992 election, fifty-three percent to forty-three percent. With a constituency that is twenty-five percent black and over fifty-nine percent female, Moseley-Braun coasted to victory in "the Year of the Woman," winning a Senate seat along with two female Senate candidates from California (Dianne Feinstein and Barbara Boxer), and sweeping into office on Clinton's coattails.

Once in the Senate, while purporting to be a liberal of the old school, Moseley-Braun began supporting Illinois business interests which had contributed to her campaign, especially the controversial food and synthetic fuel giant Archer-Daniels-Midland Corporation ("ADM," based in Decatur, Illinois) and its chairman, Dwayne Andreas. Andreas had contributed heavily to her campaign(as well as to the campaigns of prominent Republicans, including Bob Dole), and had been found to have violated campaign finance laws by the Federal Election Commission. She championed the pet projects of Andreas and ADM in the Senate, namely, federal subsidies of gasohol and other biofuels. In July 1993, she took on Jesse

Helms (R–NC) and defeated his efforts to renew a patent for the United Daughters of the Confederacy, a symbol of racism in the South.

But this modest accomplishment was soon dwarfed by Moseley-Braun's numerous campaign finance scandals that threatened to engulf her in flames.

In 1993, it was alleged that she had violated campaign laws left and right during her 1992 Senate campaign. Allegations included that one hundred-thirty-eight of her contributors had illegally exceeded the thousand-dollar campaign contribution limit, and $249,000 of her funds raised were not accounted for in campaign expenditures, and were alleged to have been pilfered by Moseley-Braun and her controversial campaign manager, Ksogie Matthews, a registered foreign agent and lobbyist for the government of Nigeria.

Matthews, who was also Moseley-Braun's fiancé in 1992, was accused of sexually harassing several female campaign workers during the campaign, and was heavily criticized for taking a month-long trip to Africa with the senator-elect after her November election.

There were many additional allegations of illegality regarding Moseley-Braun's 1992 Senate campaign. She and Ksogie Matthews were accused of cooking the books and of illegally using her campaign funds for personal items, such as clothing, travel and other personal uses. She was also accused of bad judgment in visiting Nigeria and meeting with dictator Sani Abacha in 1996, and of ignoring Abacha's human rights violations. She was also accused of being a foreign agent for Nigeria and of getting financial aid from Abacha, while serving as U.S. Senator.

Moseley-Braun was criticized by Republicans, Democrats and many officials of the U.S. State Department for making a secret trip in 1996 to Nigeria with Matthews.

The affair became more sordid in 1997 when Moseley-Braun broke up with Matthews, and he fled the country and went into hiding after failing to pay for over two hundred and fifty thousand dollars in travel expenses owed to travel agencies for trips he had taken with the senator. Matthews was sued by the agencies, which tried to subpoena Moseley-Braun to appear in court and testify as to embarrassing details of this deadbeat's actions, as well as to his whereabouts.

Matthews has never been found, disappearing into the night.

In 1997, coming under heavy criticism even from her patron saint, Mayor Richard Daley of Chicago, Moseley-Braun finally admitted, "I have erred in the handling of the whole issue of my private travel."

Meanwhile, in 1997, the Federal Election Commission audited Moseley-Braun's 1992 Senate campaign, with inconclusive results.

Also in 1997, however, the Internal Revenue Service investigated Moseley-Braun's records and tax returns dating back to her days as Cook County Recorder of Deeds (1989-92) and alleged she may have violated numerous criminal laws, including tax evasion laws. The IRS formally requested Attorney General Janet Reno to appoint and order convened two grand juries to hear witnesses under oath and to determine whether criminal charges should be brought against Moseley-Braun for tax evasion and tax fraud. Reno refused to appoint the grand juries, leading an IRS deputy director and attorney to remark that such a refusal by the Attorney General to appoint grand juries to investigate someone on the request of the IRS was "unheard of" in the twenty-eight years he has been practicing tax law.

If Moseley-Braun were forced to testify in front of a grand jury under oath, as Clinton was, it would be tempting to speculate what she would say, given her repeated contradictions and confusing mishmash of statements issued about her various and sundry scandals.

But the scandals and rumors went on and on. On September 6, 1998, nationally syndicated conservative columnist George Will wrote and published a scathing column attacking Moseley-Braun for corruption and foreign influence peddling.

On September 7, 1998, the next day, the senator publicly accused George Will of being a racist and said that she was a victim of racist efforts to unseat her in her tight reelection battle in Illinois. Attending a Labor Day celebration at the crowded Navy Pier in the Chicago Loop, Moseley-Braun angrily told reporters that "everything" in Will's nationally syndicated column was "false and racist . . . I think because he could not say 'nigger,' he said the word 'corrupt,' " (The column did not use the word "corrupt" but merely described the senator's woes). The irate senator added, "George Will should just put on his hood [a reference to the Ku Klux Klan] and go back to wherever he came from." She also indicated that she would no longer answer "any" questions about her allegedly illegal use of 1992 campaign funds for personal use or about her trip to Nigeria.

Just a few hours later on the same day, after being heavily criticized for playing the race card to deflect attention from her sins, Moseley-Braun issued an apology for losing her temper and for using language that she admitted was "not appropriate."

Will, with his characteristically snotty, pseudo-intellectual attitude, retorted that "People are weary of, and are not impressed by, such cynical name-calling. Calling her many critics 'racist' is the senator's way of trying to change the subject. But the important subject is, in the words of Martin Luther King, 'not the color of her skin, but the content of her character.' About that, the facts speak more eloquently than the senator does."

In 1998 she faced a tough, scandal-plagued re-election campaign against a well-financed right-wing Republican Illinois State Senator Peter Fitzgerald.

Moseley-Braun angrily cried out, "For more than five years, I've endured baseless charges in reckless continuation that were intended to divert attention from my solid record of achievement as a United States Senator." Appealing to the race card, Moseley-Braun attempted to motivate black voters in a race against white Fitzgerald, a tactic used by Alcee Hastings, J. C. Watts and several other African-American politicians caught in scandal webs.

Moseley-Braun's decision to play the race card

may backfire on her. Other politicians have been damaged by using such a strategy in the Land of Lincoln. In the March 1998 Illinois Democratic gubernatorial primary, the black front-runner said that he considered his opponents "non-qualified white boys."

His support evaporated overnight, and he lost the primary.

Whether that happens to Moseley-Braun also remains questionable. What is known is that win or lose, the senator faces some tough questions on the road ahead, relating to the skeletons in her closet dating back a long way.

Given the unholy alliance between political partisanship and criminal law that is developing at a dangerous pace in this country, it would be interesting to see whether Moseley-Braun would be aggressively investigated and prosecuted by a Republican Attorney General, if a Republican administration succeeds Clinton's.

Ominously, the practice of bringing the criminal law down on your political enemies, and turning a blind eye to criminal violations by your political cronies, is a dangerous new development in American politics, one which is emblematic of dictatorships around the world and throughout history.

If political credentials are allowed to act as both sword and shield in determining the long-arm reach of American criminal law, this country is in for a very rough ride ahead.

FRANK MURKOWSKI

Baked Alaska for Dessert

Senator Frank H. Murkowski has been the Republican Junior Senator from Alaska since his election in 1980. The Senior Senator, Ted Stevens, is also a Republican. Alaska has only one Representative in the House, Republican Don Young, who has won thirteen consecutive terms. In Presidential elections, Alaska has not voted for a Democrat since 1968. Clinton lost by big margins there in 1992 and 1996. The one political exception is Democratic Governor Tony Knowles, who won a three-way general election in 1994 by only five hundred and thirty-six votes.

Alaska became a state in 1959. Its huge land mass is larger than all the Northeastern and Great Lakes states combined. Its population consists of less than two-tenths of one percent of the nation, about six hundred thousand out of 265 million. While insignificant in the electoral vote that selects the President, Alaska is a powerhouse in the Congress.

The reason is the seniority system which has made Young the Chairman of the House Resources Committee, Stevens the Chairman of the Senate Appropriations Committee, and Murkowski the Chairman of the Energy and Natural Resources Committee in the Senate.

Murkowski is sixty-five and shows no sign of retiring. He is expected to be reelected for another six-year term in 1998. He grew up in Seattle and Ketchikan, served in the Coast Guard in 1955–56, spent one year at a bank in Seattle and then became a banker in Fairbanks, until his election to the Senate in 1980. He obtained a seat on the Energy Committee, which deals with issues of special interest to Alaskans, and worked his way up the minority ranking until the Republican sweep in 1994 moved him to the Chair. His Chairmanship is not only valuable to Alaska, it is the source of contributions which fuel his campaign. In his 1992 campaign Murkowski spent $1,910,000, more than twice that of his Democratic challenger.

Murkowski is at the center of the efforts of the private utility companies to deregulate the $200 billion electric power industry in the United

States, meaning that consumers will be able to choose an electric company as it can now choose long distance telephone service. While some states have already passed legislation permitting competition between powerful private utilities and local public providers, federal deregulation legislation is lagging.

The Edison Electric Institute is the lobbying group for over one hundred private utilities that provide three quarters of the country's electric power. Their competition comes from public utility systems and electric cooperatives serving rural areas which share the other quarter of the electric business. More than ninety percent of the Alaska residents are served by electric cooperatives and public power companies, so Murkowski's sponsorship of deregulation would not seem to serve his local industry. It does seem to serve Murkowski's financing needs at election time. The private companies are in a far better position to provide him with contributions than their competitors.

In the first ten months of 1996, Murkowski received over thirty thousand dollars from the private utilities' political action committees and another twenty thousand dollars of individual contributions from private utility companies and their lobbyists. In addition, the same special interests spent more than forty thousand dollars to pay

for junkets by Murkowski and his staff in some fifteen separate trips between 1996 and 1997 compared to only two trips financed by public electric
companies. Although Nancy Murkowski was not
on the Senator's staff, she accompanied her husband on a taxpayer-financed ten-day trip to Japan
and China in December 1996, for which American lobbyists and Japanese companies arranged to
pay over seven thousand dollars so that she could
go.

The largest electric utility in the southwest is
the Arizona Public Service Company, owned by a
holding company known as Pinnacle West, whose
chief executive is Richard Snell. In March 1997,
Snell testified before the Energy Committee, urging Congress to pass legislation which would bar
public utilities from marketing tax exempt bonds
unless they agreed to sell electricity to customers
only within their current service area. In November 1997, Murkowski introduced Senate Bill 1483,
which adopted Snell's position, stating that, "Public power should not obtain a competitive advantage in the open marketplace based on a federal
subsidy that flows from the ability to issue tax-ex-
empt debt." Pinnacle West's Washington lobbyist
sent a confidential memo to a dozen other lobbyists for private utilities, urging them to support

Murkowski because he appeared to be willing to lead the fight in Congress in support of Snell's position.

Murkowski has sided with the private utilities on every major issue. He is a co-sponsor with Senator Alfonse D'Amato (R–NY) of proposed legislation that would allow private electric companies to purchase a company that is far from the utility's present service area. The bill is opposed by the public power interests because they claim it would hurt consumers by letting the large companies dominate the electricity markets.

The Murkowski story is but the tip of the huge iceberg of large corporations and moneyed interests in every sector of corporate America who attain their goals because only a few in Washington want to do anything to change the system. Money is the key to re-election. The incumbents can use their offices to raise large sums, which they use to stave off challenges in primaries and general elections. Incumbents are returned to office in extremely high percentages all the time. That is the reason neither party wants the kind of campaign finance reform that Senators John McCain and Russell Feingold have proposed. Feingold is voluntarily following the guidelines of his bill in his own 1998 re-election contest, and it has become a closer race for that reason. America will not see the Murkowski pattern broken unless the voters understand what is at stake and use their votes to send a message for change.

JOHN E. PETERSON

Excessive Hugger in the House

John E. Peterson (R-PA) represents the Fifth Congressional District of Pennsylvania, in north-central Pennsylvania, in a remote area characterized by jagged mountains and narrow streams.

Peterson, born in 1938 as the son of a steelworker, grew up in Titusville, ran the Peterson's Golden Dawn Food Market from 1958 to 1984, and was elected to the House in 1996.

One of the freshest House members, Peterson is married, with children, and claims to embody solid Republican conservative family values. In his 1996 campaign, he described himself as a "country-born Sunday School teacher, a happily married grandfather and a small-town grocer" from Pleasantville. Before running for Congress, he had been a Pennsylvania State Senator for twelve years.

Peterson ran for an open congressional seat in the Fifth in 1996, and seemed a shoo-in until the *Harrisburg Patriot News* ran a story in mid-October 1996, alleging that six women had accused Peterson of sexual harassment and inappropriate sexual advances. Soon, a seventh accusatory woman surfaced.

Three of the women claimed that Peterson had kissed them against their will, a fourth claimed he had grabbed her breasts in a Harrisburg state capitol elevator when she had been a teenage State Senate page.

One of the women, Emily Gruss Gillis, had worked as associate director of the Center for Rural Pennsylvania. She claimed that in 1988, while she was twenty-six and he was forty-nine, Peterson forcibly kissed her in a hallway at the Center and pulled her toward him with a hand behind her neck, "like a prisoner."

"I offered resistance," Gillis said, "pushing back, and I felt like he overcame my resistance. My first concern was personal safety."

"I am glad that this has come out," she added, "because I think these things tend to keep happening unless someone speaks up."

Katherine Northam said that Peterson had grabbed one of her breasts in a capitol elevator in 1987, while she was a sixteen-year-old page in the

Senate, where her mother worked as a research analyst.

"I was holding a box of invitations," Northam explained, "and it was the size of a cake box. I had both of my arms extended in front of me. He said, 'What are these?' And as he said that, he grabbed my breast." Northam said she had tried to free herself from his clammy embrace by "hunching my shoulders and leaning forward." Then she ran into her mother's office when the elevator door mercifully opened. Northam eventually filed a formal sex harassment complaint against Peterson with the State Senate.

"I was embarrassed and humiliated," Northam said. "I didn't report this because my mother felt no one would take these allegations seriously. It was my word against his."

Two other women, a lobbyist and a former state employee, accused Peterson of sex harassment. The lobbyist, afraid to use her name, said he had given her "a hug and a deep-throat kiss" in his state Senate office.

Three other women said they had had to resign from Peterson's office because of "uncomfortable work situations" he had caused them.

Peterson, then fifty-seven years old, denied all the charges, and said "This never happened, it's pretty obvious that it's a political ploy to affect this election, no doubt about it . . . for it to surface three weeks prior to an election is obviously political."

But Peterson admitted, "I may have been an excessive hugger and a too friendly person. But it was never a sexual advance—never, ever, ever."

Peterson's opponent, Democrat State Representative Ruth Rudy, compared Peterson's misconduct to the infamous former U.S. Senator Bob Packwood (R-OR), who was forced out of office in 1995 after sixteen women accused him of sexual harassment. "These are very serious charges that he is going to have to answer one way or another," Rudy said.

Peterson, while denying the charges and dismissing them as "decade-old," also said, "It can haunt me forever. It is definitely a political noose around my neck. I understand that." He accused Rudy of running a "vicious whisper campaign" against him.

Peterson won the election sixty to forty percent, but the charges continued to haunt him.

In the House, he has been appointed to the Education and Workforce Committee, and he has attacked the federal government as "the greatest threat to rural health care."

He is in favor of impeaching Clinton for "inappropriate sexual relations" with Lewinsky.

CHUCK ROBB

The Senator and the Beauty Queen-Masseuse

Senator Charles (Chuck) Robb seems to have it all: handsome, intelligent, winner of the Bronze Star in Vietnam, husband of former President Lyndon Johnson's daughter, Lynda Bird (whom he married in 1967), Robb has been at the center of political life for thirty years.

Coasting from one elected high office to another, from Lieutenant Governor to Governor of Virginia, Robb ran for the U.S. Senate and was elected in 1988.

Appearing as straightlaced as any happily married family man should, supported by Evangelical Christians and conservatives alike, Robb was one of the rising stars of the Democratic Party, often touted as a Presidential hopeful, when vague rumblings of scandal began to shake his career.

As early as August 1988, a series of newspaper stories accused Robb—while Governor of Virginia—of having attended a number of "wild parties" in Virginia Beach, where cocaine and sex were in great supply.

In April 1991, NBC broadcast a story asserting that Robb was guilty of adultery. He was accused of having had a sexual affair with former Miss Virginia Tai Collins, a blond beauty he had met and had sexual encounters with for years. In October 1991, Collins posed naked for *Playboy* and gave a detailed kiss-and-tell interview about her relationship with Robb. She told of having sex, not just giving a massage, in New York's Pierre Hotel, and of Robb's having showered her with gifts and asking her out on numerous dates.

Robb denied the charges, yet his denials were countered by the words of his own Senate aides, several of whom told the *Washington Post* in 1994 that Robb "was sexually involved with at least half a dozen other women approximately twenty to twenty-five years his junior" while married and a father. Robb continued to insist that his wife was "the only woman I've loved, or slept with, or had sexual relations with." He also denied the rumors that he was a cokehead and a consort of cocaine users and dealers.

Lynda Robb stood by her man. "We will celebrate our thirtieth wedding anniversary this December," she said proudly, "and I would marry him again tomorrow."

Collins continued to surface in the news, and claimed that Robb's people had harassed her to threaten her into silence about her affair. She declared on NBC's *Expose* news program that she and Robb had been lovers since 1984, when she was twenty and Robb was forty-five. "I was just a kid," she exclaimed. "I liked the fact that everybody who is very influential and rich wanted me at the parties.

"We were two adults and both of us knew what we were doing," she says of Robb's affair with her. "We made a mistake."

Initially, Robb totally denied having had sex with her. "There was absolutely, categorically no sexual relationship whatsoever," insisting that he had a "robe on" at all times and that he had "just received a massage" from her (while wearing the robe) at the Pierre Hotel in New York. Waxing moralistic, he added, "I clearly placed myself in circumstances inappropriate for a happily married family man. I have a very understanding, forgiving wife, and three loving daughters."

Robb's pretentious denials of sex with Collins quickly led to such jokes as "If Chuck Robb was in a hotel room with Miss Virginia, he was wearing a robe, but he didn't have sex with her, then he's too stupid to be president."

Despite his denials, Robb seemed to slip from the ranks of the senatorial elite. The *Richmond Times Dispatch* immediately wrote him off as a future Presidential contender. "President Charles S. Robb? Forget it!" guffawed the newspaper in a scathing editorial.

What is especially interesting about Robb is that, with his experience in politics dating back to Johnson's heyday, why would he risk his reputation as a "family values" politician by cavorting with a sex kitten? That Robb eventually came to acknowledge a relationship with Collins, but denied the sexual details of it, is reminiscent of Clinton's later denials of an affair with Monica Lewinsky and his attempts to split words, hairs and logic by calling it an "inappropriate" relationship but denying it was "sexual."

Despite the sex and drugs scandal, Robb went on to win re-election to the Senate for a second term in 1994, and has seemed to have reached a political plateau as the U.S. Senator for Virginia.

Interestingly, if Clinton survives the Lewinsky affair, he may make the world safe for candidates like Robb, who have adulterous skeletons in their closets.

DAN SCHAEFER

A Man of Energy—for Hire?

Congressman Dan Schaefer is the Republican Representative from the suburbs of Denver, Colorado. He was first elected to the House in March 1983 to replace Astronaut Jack Swigert, who had been elected in 1982 but died before taking office. Schaefer is a solid conservative reelected every two years from the equally solid Republican 6th District. More important, he is the chairman of the Energy and Power Subcommittee of the House Commerce Committee, and makes no bones about having the energy industry tell him what it wants in return for giving money to his campaigns.

Schaefer told the *Energy Daily*: "We go to industry and we ask industry, what is it we can do to make your job easier and to help you in this competitive world we have, rather than writing legislation and having industry comment on what we write."

On two occasions he was able to restore and increase the federal funds for research and development of renewable energy. He supports the deregulation of electric utility companies.

Schaefer's approach to the industries he oversees in the House has been appreciated. For his 1996 re-election, he raised $742,000, much of it from energy companies. In April 1997, a group of natural gas companies hosted a fund-raiser for him in Washington. They like him.

Schaefer can feel safe about how to stroke the energy executives and their lobbyists. Who's to complain? One story about his colleague Dan Burton makes the point. Burton is chairman of the House Committee which is doing the investigating of fund-raising practices, but he is focusing only on the Democrats. He feels personally safe. Why? Because when Burton came under investigation over an incident with Mark Siegel in 1996, the Ethics Committee never got around to it.

Siegel was the lobbyist for Pakistan. Burton was a strong supporter of Pakistan's interests in Congress. Siegel claims Burton told him he had to contribute $5,000 for Burton's campaign. Siegel said he was a Democrat and only contributed to

Democratic Party candidates. Burton's answer, according to Siegel, "That's gonna cost you ten."

Siegel complained of extortion. The result: Burton is still going strong, Siegel's credibility has been questioned and his job is in jeopardy. And the practice goes on. Altogether the Republican Party raised $549 million during the last election cycle, compared with $332 million for the Democrats.

The Democrats in Congress, with a few Republicans like Senator John McCain of Arizona, are trying to *get* the system changed through the McCain–Feingold campaign finance bill. The Republicans are blocking it. They are trying to *get* Clinton, Gore and the Democratic Party.

Will the country see a real campaign finance reform law anytime soon? Don't count on it. Schaefer's happy. The utility companies are happy. It's just one big Party.

E. G. (BUD) SHUSTER

It's a Family Affair

The Congressman from the 9th District of Pennsylvania is Bud Shuster, a Republican first elected to the House in 1972 and now Chairman of its Transportation and Infrastructure Committee.

Shuster's 9th Congressional District lies wholly within the Appalachian Mountain chain that runs through central Pennsylvania. It has been solidly Republican for years. Shuster ran unopposed in the 1994 general election and won with seventy-four percent of the vote in 1996.

Bud Shuster is also a national policymaker on transportation and highway issues and an important player in the Republican leadership in the House. He has, however, a nagging problem about ethical and personal conduct which goes back to February 1996.

On February 29, 1996 a consumer advocacy group asked the Justice Department to investigate Shuster's dealings with Ann Eppard, a transportation lobbyist who has earned more than $1 million annually and was raising money for the 1996 Congressional campaigns of Shuster in the 9th District and his son Bob Shuster who was standing for his first election in Pennsylvania's 5th District Republican primary. Had he won that seat Bud and Bob would have become the first father-son team in the history of the United States House of Representatives. Despite Ann Eppard's fund-raising assistance, Bob received only eighteen percent of the vote in a four-way primary, losing to Representative John E. Peterson, who later admitted in the general election that "I may have been an excessive hugger" when seven women came forward to accuse him of inappropriate sexual advances.

Bud Shuster's ethics problem over Ann Eppard's activities had a sexual overtone. *Roll Call*, a Washington newspaper covering Congress, revealed that Bud Shuster frequently stayed overnight at her Washington-area home. After first telling *Roll Call* that he did not "live" at Eppard's home while in Washington, Shuster later acknowledged his regular lodging with her and indicated that he did not pay her rent. There was no requirement under the ethics rules to do so, Shuster told Gannett News Service.

When Eppard refused to answer questions, describing them as "Do you still beat your wife" questions, Shuster in a later statement said that "two or three nights a week" he would either stay in his office when working late or on special occasions his wife, family, and he would stay at Ann Eppard's home.

The Congressional Accountability Project, a wathdog public interest group, also filed charges against Shuster with the Ethics Committee about the Eppard lobbying activities and her previous twenty-five-year career as an aide to Shuster. Questions were also raised about Shuster's intervention for a developer who is a business partner with two of Shuster's sons in a Chrysler dealership.

In July 1997 the Congressional watchdog group said it had new evidence of unethical behavior: namely, Shuster's frequent combining of official fact-finding with campaign fund-raising on the same trip. They charged Shuster with giving the appearance that he requires donations from people who want him to hear their opinions on lucrative federal transportation projects.

That group criticized and charged the Republican-dominanted Ethics Committee with forestalling any effective investigation into the many complaints about Shuster's conduct.

Shuster and Eppard vigorously deny any wrongdoing, saying they adhered scrupulously to Congressional and FEC regulations. Maybe that's part of the problem.

BOB SMITH

I'll Come Back If I Can Be Chairman of the Agriculture Committee

Robert F. (Bob) Smith has served fourteen years in the House, first twelve, then a two-year gap when he chose to retire at sixty-three, and then a return to Congress under unusual circumstances.

In November 1993, before it was even thought that the Republicans would have a majority in the House, Smith announced his retirement from the 2nd District of Oregon, which had become increasingly Republican during his incumbency. Many voters in his district, which is seventy-five-percent federally owned land, are not happy with environmental activists in Washington who are forcing the timber workers out of those lands because the spotted owl was being endangered by their work.

Smith was a successful cattle rancher before he entered state politics at twenty-nine. In 1982, he was elected to the U.S. House of Representatives where he worked in the Agricultural Committee dominated by the Democratic majority. When he retired, the scramble in the 1994 Republican primary produced Wes Cooley, a businessman selling nutritional supplements, who had served two years in the Oregon State Senate and won the Congressional seat on his self-promoting slogan, "the most conservative state senator."

The primary election in Oregon was scheduled for May 21, 1996, and no one had filed to oppose Cooley for re-election, when Smith's hometown newspaper, the *Medford Mail Tribune*, claimed that Cooley had never served in the Army in Korea during the Korean War, as he had claimed on the 1994 state voter guide. Army documents showed Cooley had not gone overseas. He was also accused of lying about when he was married, so his wife could continue to collect military survivor's benefits from her former deceased spouse.

Things got worse for Cooley. He was accused of paying an employee illegally low wages and then claiming the man as a dependent on his income tax return. Cooley claimed he was innocent and refused to step down from the 1996 re-election campaign. He said, "We have very few publications in this country that are very, very conservative, that really try to report the news objectively. It is always slanted."

Cooley tried to stay in as the Republican candidate, but the Republican National Committee Chairman twisted Cooley's arm and Newt twisted Smith's arm to come back from retirement. Smith said he would do so only if he got the chair of the powerful Agriculture Committee in the House. He was assured by the House leaders. Cooley withdrew in August 1996 as he was about to be indicted.

Smith was an easy winner in 1996, and returned in Washington to concentrate on forest issues as Chair of the Agriculture Committee. Cooley is down but not out. The big loser is the spotted owl.

GERALD B. H. SOLOMON

Assault Weapons on the Hudson

Gerald Solomon has represented the 22nd District of New York in Congress since 1978. His District includes the Hudson River Valley south and north of Albany. He grew up and attended schools in New York State, after which he founded his insurance agency in Glen Falls. He now hales from the town of Queensbury.

Solomon is a strong partisan, an aggressive conservative easily angered when he is crossed. As Chairman of the House Rules Committee, he is involved in virtually every important piece of legislation in the House, controlling the agenda of which bills get brought to the floor and which bills are assigned to committees.

In May 1996, when Congressman Patrick J. Kennedy (D-RI), son of Senator Ted Kennedy, spoke of the Kennedy family's personal tragedies resulting from assault weapons, in opposing a Republican-backed bill repealing the ban on assault weapons, Solomon angrily retorted, "When he stands up and questions the integrity of those of us who have this bill on the floor, the gentleman ought to be a little more careful. And let me tell you why: because my wife lives alone five days a week in a rural area in upstate New York. She has a right to defend herself when I'm not there, son. And don't you ever forget it. Don't you ever forget it."

Solomon then challenged Kennedy to come outside the House floor and have a go at it, *mano a mano.*

Kennedy had irked Solomon by saying, "Shame on you ... play with the evil, die with the devil," and had personally "insulted" Solomon by adding, "You'll never know, Mr. Chairman, what it's like, because you don't have anyone in your family who was killed."

In attacking and bullying Kennedy, Solomon displayed the same ornery temper in 1998 when he removed the portrait of the late Claude Pepper, a respected long-term Congressman from Florida (D-FL), which had been hanging in the Rules Committee room, and replaced it with the portrait of Howard Smith, a segregationist from Virginia. It took a principled protest in January 1998 by Representative John Lewis of Georgia, a hero of the civil rights movement, and eight other members of the Congressional Black Caucus, to change Solomon's mind. Earlier, when told that what he was doing was offensive to all black people, he had said, "If we want to adorn our walls only with angels, our walls will remain bare." The downstate press called for an apology. Solomon was silent.

But he has not been silent when it comes to standing up for campaign contributors. On December 5, 1995, on the very same day when he succeeded in persuading Congress to pass a bill retaining expensive federal subsidies for the dairy industry, the National Milk Producers wrote to all the dairy lobbyists in Washington, "To show your appreciation to Senator Solomon, please join us for a breakfast . . . PACS throughout the industry are asked to contribute $1,000."

Solomon wryly noted that this was just "a coincidence," the standard "not guilty" plea to bribery charges.

Solomon's spirited 1996 defense of General Electric, whose many employees live in his District, illustrates how intimidating and effective Solomon can be. When Democratic Assemblyman Richard Brodsky of Westchester County criticized Republican Governor Pataki (a protégé of

Senator D'Amato, R-NY) for settling pollution charges against General Electric without a fine and for a meaningless promise to spend more money on environmental projects, Solomon warned Brodsky, "As Chairman of the Rules Committee, I could easily retaliate by involving myself in the activities of your assembly district."

Solomon himself, despite his bluster, does not have a clean record. In 1992, he was exposed as having written three bad checks during the House Bank Account "Rubbergate" scandal, and he pled "innocent" due to "mistake." He also accused the House Bank of "incompetence" in mishandling his misdeeds.

It is a crime to knowingly and intentionally write a bad check, knowing there are insufficient funds to cover the check.

Earlier in his career, Solomon ran into trouble with the House Ethics Committee for other misdeeds. In 1986, New York City developer Francesco Galesi (under the name "Lake George Ventures, Inc.) bought the "Top of the World" real estate complex from Solomon and six other partners.

According to a *Times-Union* news story in October 1989, as part of that 1986 sale, Solomon also bought a townhouse at the site for a low price of $135,000—at least $36,000 less than the selling price of comparable townhouses in the area. In addition, Solomon received furniture, a paint job and a finished basement in the townhouse, all worth nearly $20,000.

Solomon also got stock in the development, for which he paid with a low-interest sweetheart loan from the developer.

Solomon had a long history of official ties with Galesi and his companies. In 1985, Solomon's Congressional aides had helped Galesi's company to obtain a $690,000 HUD grant, among other favors.

House ethics rules officially state that a Congressman may not accept gifts worth more than $100 from people or companies who deal directly with Congress.

Solomon had failed to disclose the townhouse largesse sweetheart deal as a "gift," and in 1991-92 he was investigated by the House Ethics Committee for fraudulently omitting that from his disclosures in 1986.

In his defense, Solomon quibbled over the definition of "gift," and claimed that the townhouse package was not a gift. He gave the House committee "secret documents," but refused to publicly disclose them, claiming they were "confidential."

He also claimed that the decor and furnishings he had received from Galesi were given to him "in settlement over a legal dispute over damage to the townhouse when it was used as a sales model."

However, the six other former partners of Solomon claimed they themselves had not been offered any sweetheart deals by Galesi.

In March 1992, the House Ethics Committee ruled in Solomon's favor, finding these gifts were not really "gifts."

In 1989, Lake George Ventures, Inc., was sued by George Rebh, a former member of the company's marketing sand sales team on the Galesi Group townhouse involving Solomon. Rebh won two court judgments for over half a million dollars against Galesi's company, Lake George Ventures, but was told the company had no assets left.

Rebh and his attorney, Bob Ganz, alleged that Lake George Ventures had hidden all of its assets by transferring them to Rotterdam Ventures Inc., the main corporate entity in Galesi's empire.

BOB STUMP

Narrow Escape After Switching to Reagan

Bob Stump is the veteran Congressman from the 3rd District in Arizona, which extends from the western side of Phoenix to cover much of the northwestern quarter of the state. He grew up in Arizona, enlisted in the Navy in 1943 and turned to cotton and grain farming when he came home in 1946.

Stump turned to politics at thirty-one, running as a Democrat. He served continuously for eighteen years in the Arizona Legislature, first in its House and then in its Senate, the last two years as Senate President. He was conservative in his views and was referred to as a "pinto Democrat." He was elected to Congress in 1976, 1978 and 1980 on the Democratic line.

Reagan's win over Carter in 1980 was the defining political event for Stump. He voted for the Reagan budget and tax cuts and then switched to the Republican Party to reflect his constituency which had become heavily Republican with the fast growth of Phoenix and its suburbs in the southeastern corner of his District.

Stump is a quiet power in the House. He is Chairman of the Veterans Affairs Committee and the second ranking Republican behind Chairman Floyd Spence of South Carolina on the important National Security Committee dealing with defense spending. He is terse in public, doesn't even employ a press secretary and returns to his District frequently, which includes Tolleson (his home), Prescott, Kingman and the Grand Canyon, the corridor so well traveled by so many Americans and foreign tourists. He is said to spend only one weekend a year in Washington. As a divorced Congressman his private life presents little interest to tabloid gossips or Internet investigators.

His strong support for the Reagan administration got him into trouble in the 1980s, when high members of the Republican executive leadership were discovered to have funneled money from secret arms sales to Iran to the Contra rebels in Nicaragua, in clear violations of existing law. Known then and now as "Iran–Contra," the affair was investigated at length in Congress, brought down Reagan's top National Security Officer, and resulted in the appointment of independent special prosecutor Lawrence Walsh. Walsh probed to find out whether the illegal activities went to the top, namely Reagan and Bush, and he indicted their aides who, unlike Reagan and Bush, could be tried and convicted in a federal court.

Oliver North was one of those convicted (although it was overturned on a technicality) in connection with what many in Congress and in the country considered a patriotic service. Stump was reputed to be in that group. When North's notes of his activities came to light, it was revealed that Bob Stump had actually been present at meetings with North and National Security Adviser Robert McFarlane, the two men who were running the extensive illegal program over an extended period of time.

Stump's adversaries called upon Walsh to present evidence to the Grand Jury on the personal knowledge and participation of the Congressmen—such as Stump—who were identified in North's Iran-Contra notes. It was a time when statements from Reagan, Bush, Congress members and other high officials were shown to be misleading at best and lies at worst. Voices for impeachment were heard but given little credence. While the conduct was admittedly illegal, there was no desire in mainstream America or within the Democratic party to discredit the high public officials involved.

Even the active managers of Iran–Contra, who covered up for others, got off lightly. Oliver North rode his popularity into politics and the media. He is today a TV personality, appearing frequently in "hero garb" discussing his views on the Clinton impeachment crisis.

STROM THURMOND

"The Sperminator," Methuselah of the U.S. Senate

Senator Strom Thurmond (R–SC) is the "Ponce de Leon" of American politicians. At the age of ninety-four, and still a roaring lion in the U.S. Senate, the legendary senator from South Carolina claims to have found the fountain of youth.

And not only in politics.

The author had the privilege of watching Thurmond on a daily basis when he was ranking Republican on the Senate Judiciary Committee, back in 1979–80. What was most striking about the man was the contrast—some would say the hypocrisy—between his public pronouncements and his private life. I personally observed him grabbing attractive female aides by the arm, effusively hugging them, planting slurpy kisses on their foreheads and cheeks. Yes, this was a Southern

Gentleman in action—perhaps in too much action.

Senator Strom, then seventy-five and married to a former beauty queen (Miss South Carolina) one-third his age, had just sired a son. Sporting his pasted toupee in the Senate elevators as he rumbled from committee room to senate floor and back, Thurmond seemed an odd bird to succeed to the mantle of his hero Jefferson Davis (President of the Confederate States during the Civil War) as he prowled around the Capitol, disappearing into side offices with a wide assortment of young, comely Senate aides and other buxom females.

His well-earned nickname among Senate aides was "The Sperminator," and it was widely rumored that he had a secret office in the Capitol where he would regularly take young women and deflower them.

It was joked that Thurmond outdid his arch-rival, Ted Kennedy (then chairman of the Judiciary Committee) in defoliating young females (they had to be under thirty, that was a requirement), while claiming to be a moral, upright family man.

But the Sperminator had indeed discovered the Fountain of Eternal Youth in the center of the maelstrom of politics.

"Young ladies keep me young," the Sperminator often said, quite literally.

Any seventy-five-year-old man who marries a twenty-year-old is suspected of being a wolf, but the Sperminator deflected such prurient speculation by carrying his Bible and continuously preaching from the pulpit of his Senate desk that he was a champion of the family and of married life, and that he decried the "shameless, Godless, Communist, liberal lifestyle of Democrats."

But when it came to sperminizing and capturing the fountain of youth, Old Strom had surely found the secret.

In the mid-1990s, *Spy* magazine published a major exposé of Thurmond, clearly articulating the same rumors and testimony I had personally seen while in the Senate, and which scores of other aides had witnessed.

"Strom's Hideout," just off the center of the Capitol, was an unofficial tourist spot in the Capitol. Yes, here you can see what the Champion of Family values does in his off time.

But who is this Methuselah of American politics? He is the man who set an all-time record for Senate filibusters (over twenty-four hours) back in 1957 when he lobbied against a fair housing bill; a man who has crossed party lines and sexual lines with impunity; a man who claims to be an arch-segregationist and anti-fornicator while in fact living a life that can only be called a Lie of the

Century. He is, in fact, a philanderer and a miscegenator.

After the political mood of the country changed in 1965, Thurmond becamse the first senator to hire black staffers and to appoint blacks to high positions, including judgeships. He quickly dropped his "Segregation Now! Segregation Forever!" party line and opportunistically embraced integration, while paying lip service to "States' Rights."

This raises the question: was Thurmond ever really a committed racist in the first place? Or was he just a hypocritical opportunist, pandering to white racism when it was in vogue, and then switching to the other side?

"Methuselah" Thurmond was born back in 1902 in the rural town of Edgefield, South Carolina, a Deep South state where, until 1964, miscegenation between the sexes was a crime and a felony.

If Thurmond had sex with a black woman and sired a black child any time before 1964, he could have been prosecuted under the state's felony miscegenation laws. As a law-and-order citizen, Senator Strom would have been the first to urge the prosecution of anyone guilty of "the shameless bastardization of our white race," as he proudly called this crime.

South Carolina has the dubious distinction of being the first Dixie state to secede from the Union, and the site of the first shots fired in the Civil War (Fort Sumter). But that dubious distinction is exceeded only by the private actions of the Sperminator, the living godlike symbol of South Carolina for over half a century, a man who has seceded from his state's and region's official party line and government policy.

Originally an arch-racist and Democrat who ran for President of the U.S. in 1948 on the old "State's Rights Democrat Party" ticket, the Sperminator later conveniently switched to the Republican Party in 1964, when the GOP began to displace the Democrats as the dominant party in the South. As of 1998, Thurmond has spent thirty-two years as a Democrat and thirty-four as a Republican. He attended the 1932 Democratic National Convention in Chicago and voted for Franklin Delano Roosevelt. He personally knew politicians born before the Civil War, and parachuted into Normandy on D-Day in 1944.

Now the senior Republican in the Senate, Thurmond is Senate President Pro Tempore, Chairman of the Senate Armed Services Committee, and fourth in line to succeed to the Presidency.

Thurmond enjoys the avid backing of the

Christian Coalition, the Christian Right and the most conservative emblems of the Republican Party. He is the ultimate Party Man, but an opportunist at heart.

Seventy-three years ago, in 1925, Thurmond allegedly had an affair with a black woman in his hometown and fathered a black daughter in 1925. Birth records show that in 1925, a black girl named Essie Mae Washington was born.

Twenty-two years later, in 1947, when the girl was an obscure student at South Carolina State College ("SCSC"), a small, all-black school in remote Orangeburg, South Carolina, Thurmond was a Democrat occupying the governor's seat. Regularly, he ordered his state trooper chauffeur to drive his governor's limousine to the rural campus of SCSC, where he would pay a secret visit to a very secret young lady.

The black student, Essie Mae Washington, was a business major and was receiving very generous financial support from the white Governor of South Carolina.

In those old pristine days, long before the news media became voyeuristic scandal sheets, politicians were left alone in their private lives. A news reporter would never have dreamed of following Governor Thurmond to SCSC, or to report in the press that a young black student there, Ms. Washington, had a secret benefactor in the governor's mansion.

Essie Mae Washington was one of those poor souls destined to live an obscure life, and she went through that life without formally acknowledging Sperminator Strom as her father. Now deceased, her lips are sealed forever.

More interesting is the question of why Thurmond, the arch-segregationist, would have made steady payments to Ms. Washington for half a century, without acknowledging her to be his own daughter?

Could this be considered "hush money?"

Could this be a precursor of what Bill Clinton would allegedly do half a century later, in trying to get Lewinsky a job in order to keep her sexual affair with him a secret?

In 1947, Bill Clinton was a one-year-old infant in Arkansas. As Thurmond made his way around SCSC, paying his private visit to an obscure young black woman, one is tempted to wonder what may have been going through his mind. Surely, he must have known that exposure of Essie Mae as his illegitimate daughter would have spelled doom for him in South Carolina politics. If he had been hauled into a court of law, say, by the mother of his daughter for child support payments and forced to answer questions under oath as to whether he had sex with the mother (granddaughter of a slave) and had sired a black daughter, would he have answered truthfully?

Is this a fair question to ask, since Clinton is being forced to answer this question in the voyeuristic-mad media climate of the late 1990s?

Why did Thurmond single out this lucky black girl for his largesse for half a century?

The story of Strom's illegitimate black daughter has been circulating inside the South for half a century. Although Thurmond and Ms. Washington both have publicly denied that she is his daughter, and although DNA tests did not exist while Essie Mae was alive, there is considerable evidence that Strom is in fact the black girl's real daddy.

South Carolina state law shields birth records with great privacy. She grew up without a father, save for the regular trips Strom made to see her at school and, later, at home. Unlike today's sirens such as Lewinsky, Flowers and Willey, this demure young lady remained very discreet.

Frank Paine, a lawyer in Evansville, South Carolina, who was a personal friend of Ms. Essie Mae Washington when they were both students at South Carolina State College half a century ago, has said that "Throughout the time she was enrolled in State [SCSC], we'd see the [Governor Thurmond's] limo come down from time to time. The story was that he [Thurmond] helped her out whenever she had troubles about the college. She never talked about it. Everybody just assumed she was his daughter."

Robert Bell, a cousin of Essie Mae Washington's future husband, insists: "Nobody needed to talk about it. I used to tease my cousin that he had married the governor's daughter. He just laughed and said, 'Well, I wish I could get some of that money.'"

The Sperminator had provided astonishingly generous financial aid to the girl during her years while she was growing up and as a student, including loans and outright gifts. At a time when federally insured student loans (which Thurmond would later bitterly oppose) had not yet come into vogue, Thurmond bankrolled the girl through college on his own, making sure she was set for life, making sure she did not wind up as "another nigra teenage mom" on the streets.

Essie Mae moved to Pennsylvania after graduating from college and stayed far away from South Carolina for the rest of her life.

While she was alive, Washington said that Thurmond was just "a close friend of my family, a wonderful man who has helped a lot of people."

However, there is nothing from Thurmond's official South Carolina governor's records to indicate that he ever helped any other indigent black people, besides Essie Mae.

Thurmond has publicly denied making "an inordinate number of visits to the school [SCSC]" but has admitted going there, pointing out that while he was governor, he was an active member of the SCSC's board.

Robert Sherrill, who wrote a book in 1968 entitled *Gothic Politics in the Deep South*, said that the Thurmond–Washington father-daughter story was "one of the most frequently-heard rumors I've ever encountered." In 1990, *Penthouse* published another story about this. While nothing was ever proved or admitted, the rumors have never ceased.

As recently as 1996, when the ninety-four-year-old Thurmond campaigned for yet another term in his lifetime Senate seat, he was caught by reporters flirting at Clemson University, where he spotted several co-ed's and asked them, "Any of you girls want a nice warm hug?" Thurmond, who has been married two times, is now still technically married, but is known to be a swinging eligible bachelor, at the age of ninety-six. His first wife was twenty-three years his junior. After her, he married his second wife, Nancy, a former Miss South Carolina beauty, in 1969, when she was twenty-three and he was sixty-seven. He separated from Nancy in 1991, privately telling his cronies that she was now "too old" to be his lover, even though she was forty-four years his junior.

Nancy, whose entire life had been devoted to her old hubby Strom, had borne him four children (the first was born when Strom was sixty-nine), and now became severely depressed over being abandoned by the Sperminator. She turned to heavy drinking, and became a card-carrying alcoholic.

A few years ago, back home in South Carolina, a police officer arrested Nancy for drunk driving, and she showed him a wad of cash. Instead of taking it, he escorted her to the degradation of a jail cell. Strom didn't care. He had other, more important things to do.

It is interesting that a man of Methuselah Strom's background now stands to judge another "Sperminator" for exactly the same type of unbridled sexual activity that he himself has allegedly engaged in.

J.C. WATTS

The Family Values, Black Republican, With Two Illegitimate Children

The Fourth Congressional District of Oklahoma encompasses the brown hills west of Oklahoma City up to the Red River. In this steamy paradise, the political landscape is dominated by J. C. Watts, a conservative, black Republican, a darling of the Christian Right, and a former college and professional football player (in the Canadian Football League).

Watts won his congressional seat in 1994 at the age of thirty-eight. He won the seat in a vacuum: fourteen-year veteran Dave McCurdy abandoned it that year to run for the Senate and lost.

Since then, Watts has acted as "Congress's version of Clarence Thomas," a conservative black who is opposed to affirmative action, opposed to expanding the civil rights laws, and opposed to any law favoring blacks over whites.

He has refused to join the Congressional Black Caucus, claiming it is "infested" with "Democrat liberals who betray black people in America."

But for his black skin, Watts would normally be considered a classic Southern cracker, even a racist. Because he is black, however, he has been showcased by the GOP, having addressed the Republican National Convention in August 1996 as an inspirational speaker, telling the convention that "Character is simply doing right when nobody is looking." In February 1997, Watts was chosen by Gingrich to give the Republican response to President Clinton's State of the Union message, but was ignored in the avalanche of O. J. Simpson trial news. (Simpson lost his civil case for killing his wife and Ron Goldman on the same day Watts delivered his address on national television.)

Watts was elected in a district whose voters are only seven percent black, so his power base is largely white and Southern.

"I didn't come to Congress to be a black leader or a white leader, but a leader," Watts has boasted. Less charitable critics have called him "an Oreo cookie"—black outside, white inside.

Watts achieved notoriety in 1997 by calling Reverend Jesse Jackson and Washington Mayor

Marion Barry "race-hustling poverty pimps," in an op-ed piece he wrote that was published in the *Washington Post*. "They just talk about poverty, but are more concerned with just moving us to another plantation," Watts said of Barry and Jackson. "What scares them the most is that black people might break out of their racial group and start talking for themselves."

This "poverty pimps" remark led to quite a fracas, in which Jackson demanded an apology. Jackson's son, also a Congressman, got into the battle of words, accusing Watts of betraying black people and of slandering his father. Watts issued a limited apology, but maintained that "privatization, not collectivism" was the simplistic solution to the black poverty-and-crime epidemic in America.

In 1996, during his re-election campaign for Congress, Watts was accused by his opponent, Democrat Ed Crocker, of defaulting on a bank loan and of having secretly fathered two children out of wedlock twenty years earlier. Watts admitted to fathering the two children out of wedlock but denied that he had willfully defaulted on any bank loan. He won re-election easily, with fifty-eight percent of the vote.

It is interesting that Watts's personal behavior, specifically his fathering not one but two kids out of wedlock, did not seem to bother his conservative constituents one bit, nor did it bother the "family values" crowd of Republicans who showcased him to the nation at their national convention.

If we are to take Watts's own words to the convention seriously, "character is simply doing right when nobody is looking," what are we to make of his having concealed the fact of his own children for twenty years?

DAVID WELDON
Doctor in the House

David Weldon (R–FL) is a practicing physician who grew up on Long Island in New York, got his MD degree from the State University of New York in Buffalo, served in the Army Medical Corps for six years and then, in 1987, when he was thirty-four, joined a medical group in Florida. Weldon considers Newt Gingrich his "idol." He led seven hopefuls for the Republican Congressional nomination from his Cape Canaveral Space Coast 15th District and came to Congress on his idol's's 1994 sweep to victory.

Newt gave Weldon a seat on the House Science Committee and its Space and Aeronautics Subcommittee. He proved to be one of the most conservative members of the 1994 Republican freshman group. In 1996 Weldon was opposed for reelection by the Democratic nominee John Byron, who had top credentials and a record as a former Navy submarine captain.

Byron charged Weldon with being "an extremist with a narrow agenda." Both candidates spent $1.1 million on the race, but Weldon, the incumbent, was able win with fifty-one percent of the vote at the same time Bob Dole beat Clinton in the district by a five-percent margin. Weldon's strong conservative convictions could send him back to the practice of medicine.

Meanwhile in 1997, Weldon took his wife Nancy on a trip to Tel Aviv which was paid for by the American Israel Education Foundation. Cynics claim he was getting an education in Israel's space program.

Wait a moment here. Israel doesn't have a space program.

THE POLITICAL MARRIAGE

Today we know more about George Washington's and Thomas Jefferson's marriages than either their wives or their constituents knew. Marriages of successful public officials, including Presidents, have always been an endangered species more so than conventional marriages. They have come under increasing scrutiny of late.

Marriages in the United States have experienced a remarkable transformation in the half-century since women's important role in winning World War II on the homefront. The resulting examination of the feminine mystique led to an assertiveness from women's groups about gender discrimination in the workforce, then to the confrontation with sexual harassment, then the Year of the Woman in the 1992 elections, and now an "in your face" crisis about the quality of the President's marriage and whether violating his marriage vows and trying to cover it up rises to the level of an impeachable offense.

Those who seek to remove him from office, and have the constitutional power to try to bring that about, stress that President Clinton lied to the American public about an extramarital relationship and therefore he is not qualified to remain in his elected office. There is implicit in this criticism of Clinton's family values the idea that the critics themselves have never lied, and are not now lying, to the public about their own marriages, past and present.

This blatant hypocrisy of the congressmen who are leading the impeachment charge has not been lost on the voters who continue to give the President increasingly high grades no matter the torrent of salacious material illegally leaked by the Starr prosecutors and then incrementally ratcheted up by a partisan Judiciary Committee. Nor has it been lost on the supermarket scandal sheets, tabloids, gossip magazines and Internet "sludge dredgers" who are revealing such sexual hypocrisy in the cause of freedom of the press.

The response from public officials is to charge the White House with illegal conduct for a "scorched earth strategy" and direct the FBI to investigate the sources of the media's information on their private lives. Newt Gingrich's ally, Tom

DeLay, the Republican whip in the House, sought to unleash the FBI investigators on *Salon*, the Internet magazine, which disclosed the extramarital five-year affair which Chairman Henry Hyde carried on with a married mother of three young children, some thirty years ago. Mr. Hyde, who is leading the Judiciary Committee's impeachment-process and who told the Washington press with a straight face that Speaker Gingrich was not influencing his actions, admitted the affair, calling it one of his "youthful indiscretions."

Henry Hyde was hardly a youth at the time. He was a successful Illinois state official in his forties during his affair with Mrs. Cherie Snodgrass. Was he lying to the American people, misleading them or just covering up a messy marriage by deceitfully blaming it on his tender age?

The political frenzy over the "purity" issue is driving contests for Congress in close elections even where the candidates are not talking about it. In New York, the eighteen-year Senate veteran, Alfonse D'Amato, whose unstable feminine relationships have received press attention, faces the eighteen-year House veteran, Chuck Schumer, who appears often with his adoring wife and two daughters. If the Democrats can pull off an upset there and take that Republican Senate seat, it will not be unrelated to a New York preference for having Schumer voting in 1999 on impeachment charges. Schumer, a gun-control Godzilla in the House, was one of the first of the 1998 Democratic candidates to have Hillary Clinton at his side as the Republicans in the House were releasing the Grand Jury's sex documents to the public. And Bill Clinton later campaigned with Schumer.

For a long time in politics, being married was the badge of family values required of our high officials. In 1964, when Nelson Rockefeller was seeking the Republican nomination for President, he was hooted from the stage for his very public divorce and remarriage. Rockefeller never achieved national office from the electorate, becoming Vice President after Nixon resigned and Ford appointed him by virtue of the 22nd Amendment to the Constitution. Both Ford and Rockefeller were nominated by a President and took office after confirmation by a majority vote of both Houses of Congress.

If Clinton should resign or be removed, Vice President Gore would become President and his choice for Vice President would require a majority vote in a House and Senate dominated by the Republican Party. Unreal as this scenario may appear, the Republican investigating committees in the Senate and House have been demanding the appointment of an independent prosecutor to investigate Al Gore's fund-raising in 1996. His calls from the White House and attendance at a Buddhist event are seen by Republicans as impeachable offenses. It defies any sense of reality that Gingrich would seek a successive removal of both Clinton and Gore through Articles of Impeachment in 1999. Such a bizarre result would make the divorced Newt Gingrich President since he is now the one who is a second heartbeat away from the Presidency under the Constitution.

As divorce in America has become more prevalent, the qualification that a candidate for high office be happily married to his first wife has subsided. Bob Dole's successful bid for the Republican Presidential nomination in 1996 appeared to be enhanced by the visible campaigning of his attractive second wife, a former member of the Cabinet and President of the American Red Cross.

This change reflects the reality of marital status in America today. Each year two million adults are involved in divorce. Fifty percent of marriages in the United States end that way. Unstable marriages affect families everywhere. Anxieties about personal relationships persist as a primary concern in the lives of our young people, both before and after marriage.

There has been a societal transformation which is driven by changes in the roles women play in the family structure and the unrealistic expectations that both men and women have of the marriage relationship. Women are present today in the work force at every level, competing in professions and executive jobs for power and prestige. Two-income families are more prevalent, out of necessity or ambition.

Today we are at the point where staying in a marriage is simply elective. While there was a time in most states that the legal basis for a divorce was adultery, the no-fault divorce laws have made it easy for either partner to leave at any time. When high expectations meet disillusionment or conflict, the woman or the man tells the nearest lawyer, "I want out."

When Bill Clinton finally admitted that he had had an inappropriate relationship with Monica Lewinsky, there was speculation about the strength of his marriage, whether Hillary would leave him. Many concluded that it was only a matter of time. From our experience with troubled marriages, such a prediction is dead wrong.

From what we know of Bill and Hillary Clinton, their marriage falls within the same category that describes most political marriages in America. They have an unstable but satisfactory marriage which is likely to endure. As a couple they have always felt free to work on separate interests or together. They chose Arkansas to begin their strategic efforts to attain a common goal. It was, and is, their joint commitment to Clinton's political success and Hillary's active role, which set them apart from the conventional married couple.

Although they came from different family backgrounds and socio-economic strata, they shared elite educational successes which developed into a satisfactory relationship in the early years of their marriage as Clinton advanced to high state office and Hillary rose to prominence in Arkansas' preeminent law firm.

Like many couples they are occasionally disappointed, they experience hurt feelings, even conflicts, but for them the continuance of the marriage partnership is more important than the frustration. They understand that the expression of their love through sexual intimacy is not the glue which keeps the marriage intact. Each provides the other with something valuable, whether it be encouragement and support for a personal achievement, or coming forward as the other's champion when he or she is under attack.

What they have is the kind of relationship that appears to be growing in America. The satisfactions within their marriage, imperfect though it may be as faithful lovers, are preferable to the alternative without each other or with another mate.

They do not even consider divorce. They seek common ground on which to cooperate and sustain the marriage.

Such marriages—collaborative, detached but satisfactory—are not uncommon among members of Congress. The shuttling between office and home base produces an adjustment in their married lives where both parties accept verbal expressions of affection, and both make allowance for the loss of intimacy to others.

Whatever can be said about this reality, does that way of life and covering it up rise to the level of an impeachable offense? In the close contests of 1998, the voters will provide the answer.

THE POLITICAL
PERSONALITY

Basic to the theory of personality development is the recognition that an infant is born helpless in a strange world. The degree of anxiety in the child, its duration and the family dynamics play the major roles in determining his adult behavior.

The prime determinant is the child's search for security. What is striking about both Newt Gingrich and Bill Clinton is that neither one had his biological father in his life. Both had critical abusive stepfathers almost from birth. Clinton's father died in an accident before he was born. Gingrich's father gave him away for adoption when he was three.

Their family dynamic set the stage early in their lives for an unusual anxiety. In addition to the normal helplessness of a child, they lacked the warmth and love from their fathers, instead experiencing actual hostility plus the difficult adjustments their mothers had to make in their own lives. Gingrich's mother describes, even today, the manic-depressive illness which overtook her life. Clinton's mother was physically abused by his stepfather.

Growing up in this environment creates a special anxiety and the need for personal security.

To cope with this situation, the child must develop a defensive mechanism. There are different orientations that serve as such a safety device. In this example we see two different personalities emerging from that kind of childhood environment.

One is the development of a compensatory need for affection expressed by an overwhelming desire to win elections because it provides the acceptance that was missing in early life. Clinton wishes he could run again. He feels others' pain. He longs for their love. He revels in the adoration of victory.

The other defense mechanism is the feeling that the entire world is a hostile place, and the coincident development of a compensatory need for power, a pursuit of control over others. The Speaker of the House is the height of dominance over a large important group.

In some public officials we can see a bit of both orientations. In others, more affected by greater childhood anxieties, there is a dominance of one over the other.

In growing up we all have two basic needs, the need for safety and the need for satisfaction. These drives are universal but the primary determinant of personality has to do with security and the freedom from fear. The child's security is dependent almost entirely on the treatment received from the parents.

Parents can undermine the security of a child in different ways: ridicule, humiliation, punishment, erratic behavior, preference for a sibling, isolation. These are present in the family dynamic in varying degrees but are most harmful where the child instinctively knows that he is not genuinely loved by a parent.

These fundamental concepts do not warrant universal application to our public officials. There is a pattern, however, among many politicians which is observable. Their self-protective mechanisms are defenses against their anxiety. They are therefore seeking security and reassurance rather than personal contentment. We marvel at times at how our elected officials hang in there rather than quitting the fight and finding personal happiness.

They react to their repeated contests with adversaries with the orientation that they learned growing up—go for the love or go for the power and that will make you secure.

Of course there are exceptions which prove the general rule. Most of our leaders grew up in a hard life environment. We appreciate the log-cabin of Lincoln, the polio of FDR, Clinton's rise from poor beginnings.

Everyone builds their self image. In other careers the picture is flexible and can change as the individual grows. Too often our elected officials adopt a rigid self-image. This is who I am, to change is weakness. These are my fixed ideas and I must adhere to their demands.

The increasing hostility and intransigence we see in politics today are the byproducts of this personality. The intimate personal relationships both within and outside of marriage are victims of that personality. For the politician the personal flaws that we all have are magnified; he feels compelled to hide them because of his need for security. And when the flaws appear in a political adversary, the need for power and security by those who live in the same glass houses compel them to cast the first stones.

THE FUTURE OF
THE PRESIDENCY

Columbus Day 1998 was perhaps the start of a new discovery of America by embattled politicians. It began the week Congress finally took a break from the sexual skirmishing in the capital so that 435 Representatives and thirty-four Senators could go home to face the voters.

To understand the impeachment proceedings it is necessary to look more closely at the two persons who refuse to budge, Bill Clinton and Newt Gingrich. Clinton can end it all the Nixon way by resigning. But there is little chance that he will do so even if the House impeaches him and the Senate vote looks to be a cliffhanger.

Gingrich can stop the insanity by accepting Gerald Ford's recommendation that both Democrats and Republicans deliver a stinging rebuke to the President as he stands in the well of the House. Clinton, the self-styled "Comeback Kid," has the stamina to stand even that shame and then move to the rostrum to deliver his State of the Union message.

Gingrich might agree to it if the November 3rd election results clearly show a mandate for permitting the President to complete his term in office. For impeachment to go forward, a new Republican majority in the Senate will probably have to rise to sixty Senators. That would permit Trent Lott to cut off any filibuster. He would need only seven Democratic Senators to cross over in order to remove Bill Clinton. The 1998 election could be the referendum on the President which brings closure one way or the other.

The process is truly out of control because no matter how bad the damage becomes for the country, both Gingrich and Clinton are not budging. That does not bother Newt Gingrich. He will play out his personal agenda in this worldwide forum even if it threatens the safety, health and security of the people. That is how Mary Kahn described the Speaker. She is the wife of Newt's former campaign manager and she spent more than six years with him socially until the early 1980s. Gingrich himself has said that his personal agenda goes far beyond his political philosophy or material gain. He is quoted as saying "I found a way to immerse my insecurities in a cause large enough to justify whatever I wanted it to."

That is where this national deadlock has its origin. Both Gingrich and Clinton had similar paternal experiences. Bill Clinton's biological father died in an accident before he was born. His stepfather was abusive to him and to Clinton's mother as well. Neither Newt nor Bill had a father's love. Both crave the power and admiration that fill the emptiness in them. Winning big elections is the psychological remedy for it is proof that they are powerful and loved. Bill Clinton has said in his time of trouble, when the people's love for him had been placed in doubt, that he wishes he could run again.

Neither Bill nor Newt will step back from this "out of control" confrontation so long as there is another vote to show whether the American people love one more than the other.

Both men are surely not role models for our children. Yet for many Americans moral leadership has less to do with being faithful to a spouse and telling lies about it than it does with using high office to enact policies that make life better for them. By this definition both Gingrich and Clinton believe they can provide moral leadership.

History proves that we do not elect our President to be an example of our national morality. We would like them to be. But we do not expect it and it is not determinative of our voting. In this country, we have had Presidents whose personal rectitude was in doubt but who are now viewed as successful leaders: Roosevelt, Eisenhower, Kennedy. On the flip side are Presidents whose formal lives were beyond reproach but who are not remembered as leaders and were not re-elected: Coolidge, Carter, Ford.

We must ask ourselves the question: Would anyone, having the luxury of our present retrospective vantage, have turned Roosevelt out of office for a sexual dalliance? Or Washington? Or even Kennedy? Of course not. The benefits of their leadership far outstrip whatever costs their personal conduct may have exacted from the nation. Whether history will associate Clinton with these men remains to be seen, but we must not tolerate such a precedent as the case before us presumes to establish: otherwise, our next fit of pique might lead us to cast out the essential man or woman who would lead our nation through its next great trial.